MACMILLAN CULTURAL READERS

PRE-INTERMEDIATE LEVEL

COLEEN DEGNAN-VENESS
WITH CHANTAL VENESS

The United States of America

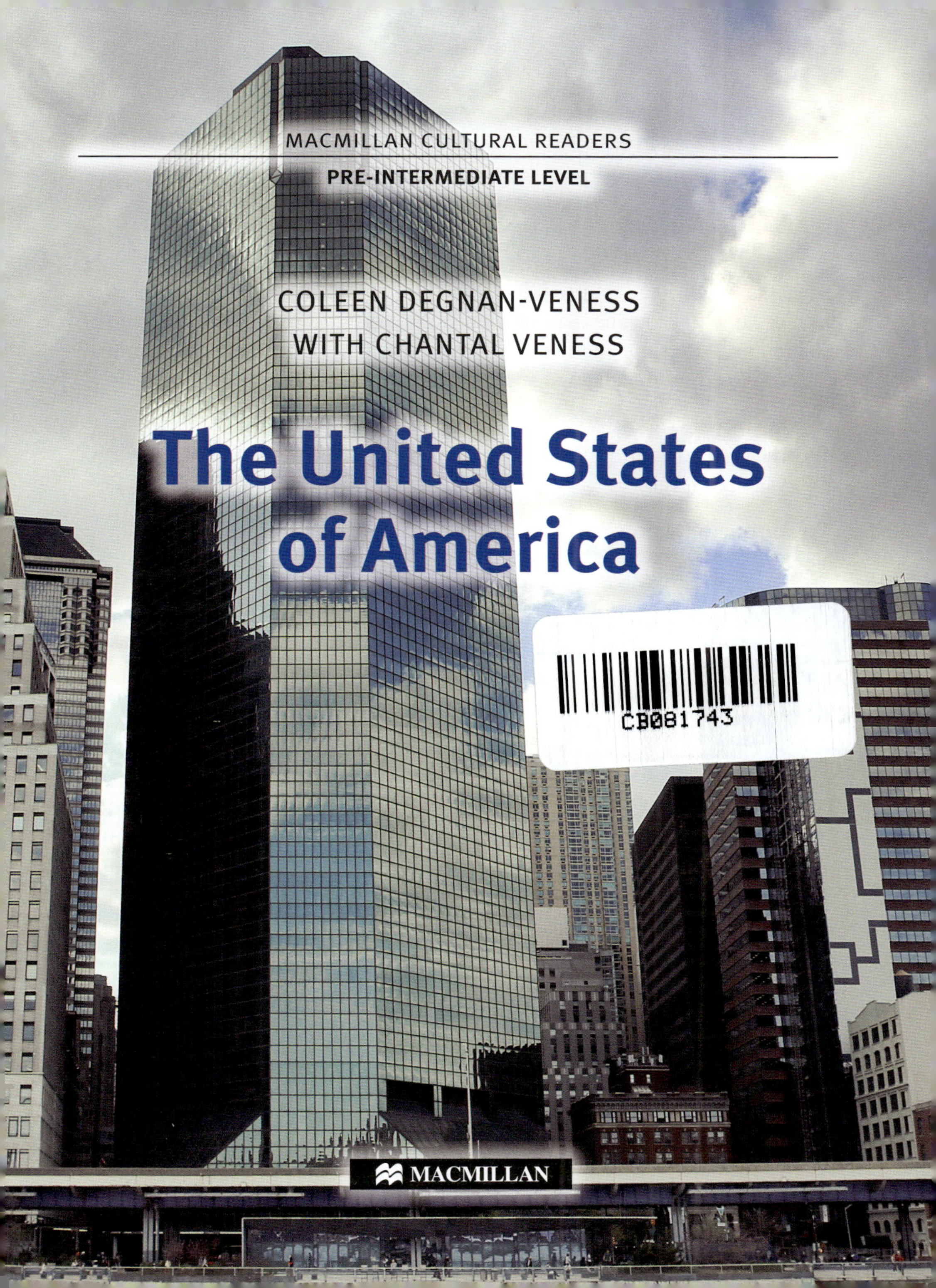

MACMILLAN

MACMILLAN CULTURAL READERS

PRE-INTERMEDIATE LEVEL

Founding Editor of the Macmillan Readers: John Milne

The Macmillan Readers provide a choice of enjoyable reading materials for learners of English. The series is published at six levels—Starter, Beginner, Elementary, Pre-intermediate, Intermediate and Upper. The Macmillan Cultural Readers are a factual strand of the series.

Level Control

Information, structure and vocabulary are controlled to suit the students' ability at each level.

The number of words at each level:

Starter	about 300 basic words
Beginner	about 600 basic words
Elementary	about 1100 basic words
Pre-intermediate	about 1400 basic words
Intermediate	about 1600 basic words
Upper	about 2200 basic words

Vocabulary

Some difficult words and phrases in this book are important for understanding the text. Some of these words are explained in the text, some are shown in the pictures, and others are marked with a number like this: [3]. Phrases are marked with [P]. Words with a number are explained in the *Glossary* at the end of the book and phrases are explained on the *Useful Phrases* page.

Answer Keys

Answer Keys for the *Points For Understanding* and *Exercises* sections can be found at www.macmillanenglish.com/readers.

Audio Download

There is an audio download and ebook available to buy for this title. Visit www.macmillanenglish.com/readers for more information.

Contents

	The Places In The Book	*4*
	Welcome To The United States Of America	*6*
1	Freedom	*8*
2	The USA Today	*16*
3	Traditions and Holidays	*20*
4	Cities and Sights	*26*
5	Nature and the Environment	*34*
6	Daily Life	*43*
7	Sports	*48*
8	Entertainment	*53*
9	American Heroes	*60*
10	Looking Forward	*69*
	Points For Understanding	*73*
	Glossary	*77*
	Useful Phrases	*84*
	Exercises	*85*

The Places In The Book

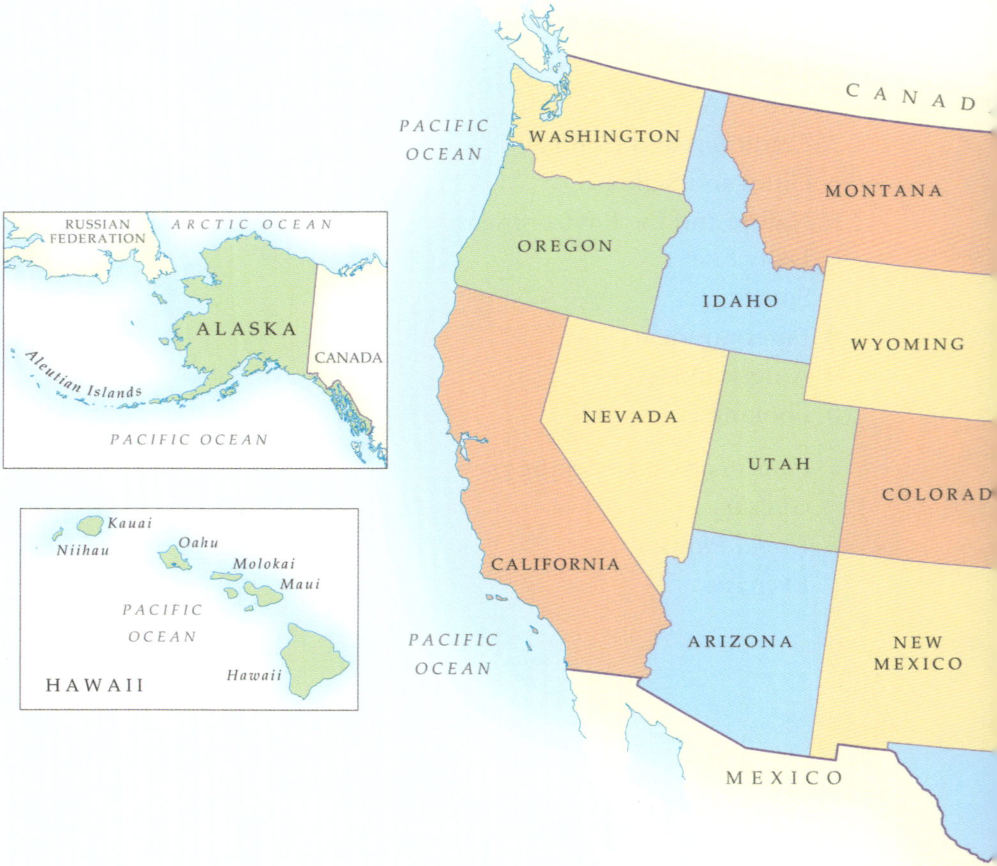

CANADA
NEW HAMPSHIRE
VERMONT
MAINE
ATLANTIC OCEAN
ORTH KOTA
MINNESOTA
WISCONSIN
OUTH KOTA
MICHIGAN
NEW YORK
MASSACHUSETTS
RHODE ISLAND
CONNECTICUT
BRASKA
IOWA
PENNSYLVANIA
NEW JERSEY
ILLINOIS
OHIO
DELAWARE
INDIANA
WEST VIRGINIA
MARYLAND
WASHINGTON D.C.
KANSAS
VIRGINIA
MISSOURI
KENTUCKY
NORTH CAROLINA
TENNESSEE
OKLAHOMA
ARKANSAS
SOUTH CAROLINA
MISSISSIPPI
ALABAMA
GEORGIA
ATLANTIC OCEAN
EXAS
LOUISIANA
Gulf of Mexico
FLORIDA

Welcome To The United States Of America

The United States of America (the USA) is a very big country: the rivers and mountains are big, and the population[1] is big. There are big cities, a lot of big houses and big cars. People have big dreams, too. Everyone wants to live "the American Dream"—the idea that anyone who works hard can become successful[2] and rich. It is a dream that really happens for some people, but it happens more often in movies and books. Many immigrants[3] have gone to the USA hoping they will become one of the lucky ones.

Almost all Americans understand that they live in a country with a very interesting history and are proud[4] of their traditions[5]. They celebrate[6] special holidays like Thanksgiving Day and the 4th of July with parades[7] and fireworks[8], which millions of people watch on TV.

The big national sports are also watched by millions on TV. American football and baseball are the most popular US sports. And because most Americans love success, they really celebrate when their team[9] wins. The best sports people become national heroes.

To other people, Americans can sometimes seem loud, proud, and a little crazy, but millions of visitors go to the USA every year and many people return again and again. This book will take you on a journey from the discovery[10] of the New World over five hundred years ago to the present day. From the wild forests to the busy cities, welcome to the United States of America.

i

Size of USA: over 4,000 kilometers from east to west
Population: more than 300 million
Capital city: Washington, D.C.
Number of states: 50 (48 mainland + Alaska and Hawaii)
Longest river: Mississippi–Missouri River 5,970 kilometers
Highest mountain: Mount McKinley, Alaska 6,194 meters

i

The US flag has thirteen white lines, or stripes, that represent[11] the thirteen colonies[12]; the fifty stars represent the fifty states.

Warm-up Quiz

How much do you know about the USA or think you know? Try these quiz questions and then read on to check your answers.

1 Which city was called New Amsterdam until 1664?
   a Miami
   b New York
   c Los Angeles

2 Which language does the largest number of immigrants speak?
   a Chinese
   b Spanish
   c Polish

3 In which month do Americans celebrate Thanksgiving Day?
   a November
   b July
   c February

4 What color are the buses that take many US children to school?
   a green
   b yellow
   c blue

5 Where is the center for US space exploration, NASA?
   a San Francisco
   b New York
   c Houston

6 Which sport is played on ice?
   a baseball
   b soccer
   c hockey

7 What game is played on Super Bowl Sunday every year?
   a football
   b basketball
   c baseball

8 Which North American wild animal is like a dog?
   a groundhog
   b coyote
   c turkey

9 Which type of music started in America at the beginning of the 20th century?
   a jazz
   b rock and roll
   c soul

10 Where is the home of US country music?
   a Boston
   b Nashville
   c Washington, D.C.

1 Freedom[13]

George Washington

George Washington

Born: February 22, 1732 Westmoreland County, Virginia
Died: December 14, 1799 Mount Vernon, Virginia
Schools: studied at home
Career: landowner, soldier, general and commander-in-chief of the colonial army, first president of the USA
Owned: Mount Vernon, one of Virginia's most important plantations; more than 100 slaves

In the fifteenth century, the richest European countries wanted to find new water routes to Asia because they wanted to trade—buy or sell things—with other countries and become richer. King Ferdinand and Queen Isabella of Spain sent explorers—men looking for new lands and routes for ships—across the oceans to find a western route to Asia. One of these men was the explorer Christopher Columbus, born in Italy, but who worked for the Spanish king and queen. He arrived in the Bahamas, islands southeast of Florida, on October 12, 1492. There he met people who painted their bodies and wore animal skins. He called the native[14] people "Indians" because he thought he was in India, and they continued to be wrongly called Indians for more than four hundred years. Today they are called Native Americans.

1565	1607	1609	1613	1619	1620
The Spanish settle Saint Augustine (Florida).	The English settle Jamestown (Virginia).	The Spanish settle Santa Fe (New Mexico).	The Dutch settle along the Hudson River (New Amsterdam, later New York).	Slaves arrive from Africa.	The English settle Plymouth (Massachusetts).

Seven years later, in 1499, another Italian explorer working for the Spanish sailed along the coast of South America. His name was Amerigo Vespucci, and this is where the name "America" comes from.

In 1609, an Englishman called Henry Hudson became the first explorer to sail up a river that is now the Hudson River in New York City. He worked for a large trading company called the Dutch East India Company, and soon after this Dutch people began to settle[15] on the new continent.

At the same time, Europeans also went to Africa to buy people. These people were then shipped to North and South America and sold to farmers. When the Africans arrived, they became slaves—people without freedom—who had to work for no money and do what they were told[P]. They had to work very hard on the coffee, tobacco[16], cotton, and sugar plantations, which were very large farms. Some worked in white people's houses, where they cooked, cleaned, and took care of children. More than ten million Africans were shipped to America over three hundred years. Families could not stay together, and so husbands lost wives and parents lost children. The slaves did not go to school, so most of them could not read or write. Their lives were very hard. Some slaves were owned by people who were kind, but many were not.

People went to North America for different reasons. One hundred and two people left England for the new continent because they wanted religious[17] freedom. These people were known as Pilgrims and they arrived in 1620, on a ship called *The Mayflower.*

The place where they first arrived became a very important symbol[18] in the history of the country's fight for freedom. The rock that they first walked on, in Plymouth, Massachusetts, is called Plymouth Rock. Life for the Pilgrims was difficult. The weather was very cold and there were dangerous wild animals. Many people died. But the Pilgrims could own land and live better lives than they had in Europe. At the end of the first year, the local people—the Native Americans—and the English settlers celebrated with a large meal together to give thanks that they were still alive.

Pilgrims from *The Mayflower* arriving at Plymouth Rock

At first, the Native Americans were happy to help the settlers. They taught them how to grow native plants for food and medicine, where to find wild animals for meat, and how to use animal fur for clothes. But the relationship between the Native Americans and settlers changed when more and more settlers arrived and took more land. There were terrible wars between the Native Americans and the settlers.

In 1624, the Dutch settled New Amsterdam on the Hudson River. Later, in 1664, King Charles of England gave orders to his men to take New Amsterdam from the Dutch. The Dutch settlers were unhappy with the Dutch government[19], so they did not fight very hard when King Charles's brother, the Duke of York, took the settlement from them. He then changed its name to New York.

In the eighteenth century, there were thirteen colonies on the east coast of the continent. England, at that time the richest and strongest country in the world, ruled these colonies. The thirteen colonies later became these states: Maine, Massachusetts, New Hampshire, Connecticut, New York, Pennsylvania, New Jersey, Maryland, Delaware, Virginia, North Carolina, South Carolina, and Georgia.

By 1763, King George the Third and his British government expected the colonists to help British soldiers living in the colonies. The colonists had to give the soldiers food and a bed. This was expensive, and the colonists were very unhappy. The British government also expected the colonists to pay taxes[20] on tea, coffee, wine, and sugar.

On December 16, 1773, about one hundred colonists decided to show King George what they thought of his tax on tea. They went to Boston Harbor at night, where there were three British ships full of tea. The men dressed as Native Americans and threw all of the tea into the water. In American history, this important event[21] is known as the Boston Tea Party. King George was angry and he closed Boston Harbor. The colonists began to prepare for war against[22] England.

One colonist, Thomas Jefferson, wrote a very famous document, called the Declaration[23] of Independence[24]. In it, he said that the colonies were a new and independent country. On July 4, 1776, Thomas Jefferson, John Adams and some other men signed[25] the Declaration of Independence at Independence Hall in Philadelphia, Pennsylvania. In the Declaration of Independence, Jefferson wrote, "All men are created equal[26]" and he wrote about man's right[27] to life, liberty (freedom), and happiness. Men on horses took the document to colonial towns and read it to the people. Now King George was angrier than ever with the colonists, and he sent more soldiers with guns across the Atlantic Ocean to New York. General George Washington and his army of colonists were waiting for them. France and Spain joined Washington and the colonists in the long American War of Independence against Britain.

Many people died in the American War of Independence. But in 1783, the war ended and a new country was born: the United States of America.

> *All men are created equal.*

Thomas Jefferson, in the Declaration of Independence

Thomas Jefferson

Born: April 13, 1743 Shadwell, Virginia
Died: July 4, 1826 Monticello, Virginia
Education[28]**:** College of William and Mary
Career: lawyer, historian, started the University of Virginia, third president of the USA
Owned: several plantations and about 200 slaves

Benjamin Franklin

Born: January 17, 1706 Boston, Massachusetts
Died: April 17, 1790 Philadelphia, Pennsylvania
Schools: school for one year, taught by his older brother
Career: writer and printer of newspapers, inventor, wrote against slavery

The people were no longer colonists; they were Americans. Some colonists who did not want independence, and who fought with the British army against their colonial neighbors, escaped to Britain or Canada.

George Washington, Benjamin Franklin, and other important colonial leaders[29] wrote the Constitution of the United States of America in 1787. The Constitution is the government document that said that the new government was a democracy[30], a government "of the people, by the people,

The signing of the Declaration of Independence

and for the people." George Washington became the first president, and John Adams was his vice-president[31].

The USA grew larger by buying land from other countries and by winning land in wars. In the north, cities grew quickly, and trade and business made many people rich. In the south, there were lots of big farms, and farming made many people rich there. Between 1793 and 1861, over eight hundred thousand slaves were sent from the northern states to the south to work on farms. Africans continued to be slaves for many more years. Slavery did not end until another war was fought—the American Civil War—a war between the states of the north and the south. After this war ended in 1865, slaves were free, and some African-American men worked in the government. But it took almost one hundred years before African-Americans had equal rights in the USA.

Life in the USA also continued to be very bad for the Native Americans. Many died trying to protect[32] their land and their families, but they were losing the fight. In 1831, the US government had started to move Native Americans to reservations—pieces of land for Native Americans only—so that they could take their land. The long journey to the reservations, often in very cold weather and without food, killed many men, women, and children.

Native American tribes

The Iroquois Nation is a group of six Native American tribes (the Cayuga, Mohawk, Onondaga, Oneida, Seneca, and Tuscarora) that have lived together under one law in New York State for hundreds of years. James Fenimore Cooper wrote about these warriors in his famous book, *The Last of the Mohicans*. (A Mohican is a person in the Mohawk tribe.)

The Lakota Sioux tribe lives in the area that is now Minnesota, Wisconsin, North and South Dakota, and part of Nebraska. In the past they had lived near the Great Lakes further east, but as more European settlers arrived, they had to move west. There are seven Sioux tribes in total.

Sitting Bull

Sitting Bull, a brave[33] leader of the Lakota Sioux tribe[34], brought many tribes together to stop the US army from taking their land in South Dakota.

When General George Custer and the US army arrived at Little Big Horn on June 25, 1876, Sitting Bull was waiting with two to three thousand tribesmen. General Custer and 267 soldiers were killed that day.

The US government sent thousands more soldiers. They wanted Sitting Bull to tell his tribes to stop fighting. Sitting Bull left and went to Canada. When he returned to the USA, he stopped fighting the US army. On December 15, 1890, Sitting Bull was killed when US police officers tried to take him to prison. Two weeks later, the US army went to Wounded Knee, South Dakota, and killed one hundred fifty Lakota men, women, and children.

1827	1861	1861–1865	1890	1924
Slavery is against the law in New York State.	Abraham Lincoln becomes the sixteenth president.	American Civil War.	US army kills over one hundred fifty Lakota Sioux Indians at Wounded Knee.	Native Americans get full citizen rights.

The USA has always been a country with a lot of immigration. After the Civil War, many Americans left their homes in the east and went to western states, where they could buy cheaper farmland. Another twelve million immigrants, many from the south and west of Europe, arrived between 1892 and 1924.

People wanted to live "the American Dream", the idea that those who work hard could find success and get rich. In 1850, there were fewer than twenty millionaires in the USA, but by 1900, there were forty thousand! The 1920s were a time of wild spending and a lot of fun for many Americans.

But on October 24, 1929, everything changed when there were terrible financial problems and the US dollar crashed. The years that followed are known in history as the Great Depression, which left many thousands of people without money, jobs, homes, or food. By 1933, millions of people had no work and they wanted a new president. President Franklin D. Roosevelt was that man, and he promised to help Americans find jobs. Roosevelt spent government money on programs for rebuilding the country. American workers got jobs building roads, airports and schools, and by 1943, nine million Americans were better off[P].

2 The USA Today

Barack Obama and his family

Today, the USA is home to many people from different races[35] and ethnic[36] groups. Since the early settlers, Americans of different races have married and had children. In 2000, seven million Americans said that they were of more than one race. Americans today come from every corner of the world, with Hispanics—people from Spanish-speaking countries—the fastest-growing ethnic group. In 2009, one in seven new marriages was between people of different races or ethnic groups, and "mixed-race" is one of the fastest-growing groups in the country. In 2008, Americans voted[37] for their forty-fourth president and chose Barack Obama, the first African-American to get the job. Obama's father was from Kenya and his mother was a white American woman from Kansas.

In the 19th and 20th centuries, when immigrants started their new lives in America, most of them learned English. English continues to be the main language, but there are over thirty-five million people who speak Spanish at home. This is because the largest number of immigrants to the USA comes from Mexico, a Spanish-speaking country south of the USA. In 2010, more than sixteen percent of the population were Hispanic.

There are over three hundred million Americans, but today only around two million of the population are Native Americans. They have many different tribal languages, but nearly all speak English. There are 310 reservations on only a little more than two percent of the land in the USA. Native Americans are citizens of the USA and they can vote, but they also have tribal laws and tribal leaders. On the reservations, children go to schools where they are taught both in English and in their tribal language.

Religion is very important to a lot of people in the USA, with about seventy-eight percent of the population Christians, about five percent other religions, and about sixteen percent who have no religion. About 1.7 percent of the adult population are Mormons and another 1.7 percent are Jewish. The number of Muslims in the USA has grown to over two-and-a-half million, as more immigrants arrive from South Asia, the Middle East, and Africa.

The USA is a society with lots of different cultures.

Something else that is important to Americans is their car. Americans are people on the go[P] and their cars are very important to them. In 2008, there were almost one hundred and forty million cars and nearly eight million motorcycles on the roads. With seventy-five percent of the population living in suburbs[38], people need their cars to go to work, to the stores, to church, and to school.

Cars are very important for Americans.

The age when people can learn to drive is different from state to state. In South Dakota, teenagers can start driving when they are only fourteen years old; in New Jersey, teenagers have to wait until they are seventeen. But for the first time since the 1950s, fewer teenagers now want to have cars, because gasoline[39] is becoming more and more expensive.

The amount of money that people earn[40] is different from state to state. On average[P] in 2010, workers in New Hampshire, New Jersey, and Connecticut earned the most, at an average of $65,000 a year. In a poorer state, like Mississippi, the average worker earned only $35,693. In 2010, twenty percent of the population of Mississippi were living in poverty[41].

The local governments of most states fix a minimum wage—the lowest pay a worker earns for one hour's work. The difference between states is surprising. There are five southern states that have no minimum wage, so some people work for very little money. In 2010, the minimum wage in the state of Washington was $9.04, while in Georgia and Wyoming it was only $5.15.

2010 Most Violent Cities

Number of violent crimes per 100,000 people in population	
Detroit, Michigan	1,111
Memphis, Tennessee	1,006
Springfield, Illinois	855
Flint, Michigan	827
Anchorage, Alaska	813

Poverty brings many problems, and, in a country where many people have guns, it can lead[42] to violent[43] crimes. When the country was new, and settlers had to worry about wild animals and fighting Native Americans, many people thought guns were necessary. The Constitution says that people have the right to own a gun. Today, many Americans would like to change the laws on owning guns. But there is also a very strong group of Americans who say that this is their right. The number of people killed by guns in the USA in 1993 was the highest ever recorded[44] at 17,075. In 2005 the number was down to 11,346.

Is the USA a dangerous country? It is in some places. But between 2007 and 2010 the number of violent crimes in the country fell. The number of crimes in New York City, once a very dangerous city, fell by sixty-two percent, after Mayor[45] Giuliani worked hard to make his city a safer place to live. By 2003, the mayor's plan had worked, and New York was one of the safest large cities in the USA.

3 Traditions and Holidays

A firework display[46] in Manhattan on the Fourth of July

Independence Day is one of the most important holidays in the USA. It is also called "the Fourth of July" because that is when it is celebrated. The holiday remembers the 4th of July 1776, when the Declaration of Independence was signed. It is a day to spend with family and friends at home, on the beach, in public parks, or at a baseball game. After dark, fireworks light up the sky all across the country. The biggest firework displays are in big cities, like Boston and Washington, D.C., which are shown on TV.

Americans are thankful for their rich farmland and celebrate their harvest[47] festival on Thanksgiving Day every November. In 1621, after their harvest, fifty-three Plymouth settlers shared a big meal with the Native Americans, and the tradition of Thanksgiving dinner was born[48]. In 1863, President Abraham Lincoln made Thanksgiving Day a national holiday celebrated on the fourth Thursday in November. Today, people eat turkey with cranberries, and native vegetables like sweet potatoes, corn, or squash, followed by apple pie or pumpkin[49] pie. Many people do not have to work on the Friday after Thanksgiving, so it is a four-day weekend. This makes it possible for people to travel home to their families for the holiday.

A traditional Thanksgiving meal: turkey, cranberries, squash, pumpkin soup and pie

Christmas is celebrated a month after Thanksgiving, on December 25th. Christmas is a Christian holiday to celebrate the birth of Jesus Christ, who Christians believe is the son of God. For about a month before, people send each other Christmas cards that say "Merry Christmas and Happy New Year". Some people prefer cards that say "Happy Holidays". Nearly everybody celebrates with a Christmas tree and presents that they put under the tree. Some people go to church on the night before Christmas, called Christmas Eve, and when they return home, they open their presents. Others open their presents on Christmas Day. The Christmas meal is usually a big bird, like turkey or goose, but some people eat roast beef because they ate turkey a month earlier for Thanksgiving. Pies, cakes, and cookies are central to Christmas celebrations. Many homes and businesses are decorated[50], inside and outside, with colored lights and other Christmas decorations, including Christmas trees. Towns and cities have competitions[51] for the house with the best decorations.

On the night of December 31st, New Year's Eve, Americans celebrate the end of the past year and the start of the New Year. Every year since 1907, a 315-kilogram ball is dropped from a flagpole[52] at 1 Times Square in New York City. Nearly one million people go there to watch it, while millions more watch it on TV. When the ball drops at midnight, the New Year begins!

Super Bowl Sunday is in January or early February. It is the day when the two best American football teams play against each other. Over one hundred million Americans sit in front of their TVs to watch the game. At half-time, when the players leave the football field in the middle of the game, famous singers entertain the people in the stadium. Is it a national holiday? Americans think it is!

Americans in the cold north wait excitedly for Groundhog Day on February 2nd. The groundhog—a small animal that lives underground—lets people know how long winter will continue. If there are clouds, the groundhog will come out of his hole. This means winter will end soon. But if it is sunny, he will go back underground and winter will continue for six more weeks. Punxsutawney, Pennsylvania, is where many people go to watch for the groundhog's message.

Valentine's Day, on February 14th, is a celebration of love and marriage. On that day, many Americans buy flowers and chocolates for the person they love. Children give valentine cards to their special friends in school. This holiday is celebrated in many countries around the world.

Another Christian holiday is Easter, which is on a Sunday in March or April. On Easter morning, children look for their Easter baskets full of chocolate animals and chocolate eggs, which their parents have hidden. At the White House in Washington, D.C., where the president lives, families are invited to play games outside on the grass.

The last Monday in May is Memorial Day. This is a day to remember the men and women who have died fighting for their country. There are parades in towns and cities across the country.

The traditional end to summer is Labor Day, a national holiday that is always on the first Monday in September. Labor Day was created in 1882 to give workers, also called laborers, a day off work. There are parades and picnics, and the beaches are full of people enjoying a three-day weekend. Football season also begins on Labor Day and goes on until Super Bowl Sunday.

One of America's favorite traditions is celebrating Halloween on October 31st. Children wear special clothes, so that people are frightened of them. They go to their neighbors' houses and when they open the door, the children shout, "Trick or treat[P]?" The neighbors usually give them candy[53], but sometimes the children play a trick on them[P]. Many people decorate their houses with pumpkins with a face cut out and a candle inside, called

Children "Trick or treating" on Halloween

jack-o-lanterns, and other Halloween decorations. Halloween is also celebrated in many other countries, like Britain and France.

There are special holidays to celebrate the lives of people who are important in the history of the USA. The second Monday in October is Columbus Day, which celebrates the life of Italian explorer Christopher Colombus. Italian–Americans organized the first Columbus Day celebrations in 1866, in New York City. The three states that do not celebrate this holiday are Alaska, Hawaii, and South Dakota. Some people think that Columbus's "discovery" of America should not be celebrated. This is because Columbus was not the first person to arrive in North America; Native Americans had already been there for thousands of years.

President George Washington's birthday and Abraham Lincoln's birthday were two different holidays in February. But in 1971, President Nixon decided they should be one holiday called Presidents' Day. It is celebrated on the third Monday in February.

3

Martin Luther King, Jr. Day is the newest holiday, which Americans started celebrating in 1986. Martin Luther King, Jr. was an African–American church leader who fought for equal rights for America's black community[54]. He was an inspiring[55] leader and his "I Have a Dream" speech is widely known around the world. He was killed on April 4, 1968. King and other black leaders worked very hard to improve life for African–Americans. As a result, President Johnson, with King next to him, signed the Voting Rights law on August 6, 1965. After that, all African–Americans had the right to vote.

Martin Luther King, Jr.

Traditions bring people together to celebrate, sing, play music, eat special food, and have a day off work. But on Martin Luther King, Jr. Day it is a little different. The day has a slogan[56], "A day ON, not a day OFF," which means it is a day to work, not a day away from, or off, work. Americans, of all races and ethnic groups, celebrate the life of this great American by working for free in their community. People plant trees, paint homes for poor people, and take food and winter clothes to them. Many people go to church and community centers, where they listen to Dr. King's speeches or talk about his work. There are parades in some towns and cities.

There is also a tradition to celebrate other cultures in America. One of the first to be celebrated was St. Patrick's Day on March 17, 1762, when Irish soldiers had a parade in New York City. St. Patrick, who was born in Britain in the late fourth century, took the Christian religion to Ireland. When almost two million Irish immigrants arrived in the USA in the late 1840s, they brought their tradition of celebrating St. Patrick. Today, people celebrate Irish culture with parades, music, and dancing. Americans, and not only Irish–Americans, wear green clothes, drink green drinks, and eat green food! Even the Chicago River is colored green for St. Patrick's Day.

Cinco de Mayo (Spanish for 5th of May) is a celebration of Mexico's independence and of Mexican culture. Mexican food is very popular in the USA, and many people enjoy Mexican music and dancing on this day.

Another tradition is to celebrate the history, culture, and traditions of different ethnic groups for a month. The ethnic history months are important in schools, where students are taught about the history of the people who made the USA a country of many cultures. It is a time to remember the people from other cultures who fought for the freedom and rights that Americans enjoy today.

February: African–American History Month
March: Irish–American Month, Greek–American Month
April: Arab–American Month, Scottish–American Month
May: South Asian–American Month, Haitian Month, Asian–Pacific Month, Jewish–American Month
June: Caribbean–American Month
July: French–American Month
September: Hispanic Month and German–American Month (Sep 15—Oct 15)
October: Filipino–American Month, Italian–American Month
November: Native American and Alaska Native Month

4 Cities and Sights [57]

Skyscrapers in New York City

The five largest cities by population in the USA are New York City, Los Angeles, Chicago, Houston, and Philadelphia. The capital city, Washington, D.C., is home to the president and the country's government.

Other names for these cities:

New York—the Big Apple
Los Angeles—L.A.
Chicago—the Windy City
Houston—Space City
Philadelphia—Philly
Washington, D.C.—D.C.
Boston—Bean Town (famous for Boston baked beans)

Boston, Massachusetts, is one of the country's oldest cities and holds a special place in the country's history.

America's urban[58] areas are not all the same, in fact, they are very different. Environment, climate[59], and the many different people living together create new tastes, sights, and sounds. Visitors to the USA are always surprised by the long distances[60] between cities. But the journey from one city to another is made quicker by the excellent roads and the many flights that travel across the country.

New York

New York City is also known as "the city that never sleeps" because something is happening 24/7[61]. Over forty-eight million visitors go there every year and spend over thirty billion dollars. New York is always busy day and night, with twenty-four-hour restaurants, stores, gyms, and coffee bars. This exciting city is an international financial and cultural center made up of five smaller towns, called boroughs. They are Manhattan, the Bronx, Brooklyn, Queens, and Staten Island. Manhattan, the smallest borough at twenty-two kilometers long and only three-and-a-half kilometers wide, is where most visitors go first. Manhattan has theaters on Broadway, shopping on Madison Avenue, art galleries in Soho, and museums[62] on Museum Mile.

New York's Best Sights

Museums: Guggenheim Museum, Metropolitan Museum of Art (third most visited in the world), American Museum of Natural History, Whitney Museum of American Art (more than 11,000 works of art)
Park: Central Park with 340 hectares[63] of grass, trees, gardens, a zoo, playing fields

With the city's long history of immigration, its population has grown from less than twenty-two thousand people in 1771 to more

New York's Tallest Skyscrapers

1899	1908	1909	1913	1929	1931	1973
Park Row Building 118 meters	Singer Building 186 meters	Metropolitan Life Insurance Tower 214 meters	Woolworth Building 241 meters	Chrysler Building 319 meters	Empire State Building 381 meters	World Trade Center 415 and 417 meters, rebuilt in 2013 at 541 meters

than eight million people today. The East Side of New York became America's first "melting pot"—an area with a large number of people from different ethnic groups all living together. Most immigrants learn to speak English, but many continue to speak their own languages at home. This means that today in New York, about eight hundred languages are spoken.

New York streets, sidewalks, and subways are most crowded at rush hour, from about 6 am to 9 am and 4 pm to 7 pm. But New Yorkers living on Staten Island can enjoy the sun on their way to work by taking the Staten Island Ferry across Upper New York Bay to Lower Manhattan, or downtown. This large boat offers tourists a free one-hour ferry ride in New York Harbor to see the sights and go past the Statue of Liberty and Ellis Island.

Many New Yorkers and tourists also use taxis to get around the city. Most tourists agree that riding from downtown Manhattan to Upper Manhattan past Central Park in a yellow taxi is a great New York experience.

The Statue of Liberty was a gift from the French to the USA in 1885.

Los Angeles

Los Angeles is home to almost four million people.

Four thousand eight hundred kilometers across the continent to the west is Los Angeles, California. More people live in California than any other state, and almost four million live in the city of L.A. The city is one of the largest financial centers in the world today. As a cultural center, L.A. offers wonderful museums of art, like the Getty Museum, which has some of the world's most famous paintings. L.A. also has sunny weather and beautiful beaches. Angelinos, as the people are called, are proud of their ethnic diversity[64].

California Facts

September 4, 1781	1781–1822	1822–1848	1848–1850	1848	1850	1892
first Spanish settlement	governed by Spain	governed by Mexico	governed by USA	gold was discovered	became the 31st state	oil was discovered

Los Angeles is famous for its movie industry[65], and many of Hollywood's movie stars and TV actors live there. At Universal Studios, the oldest and most famous of the movie studios, visitors can see how movies are made.

But L.A. is not just a city for movie stars. The growing difference between rich and poor people in L.A. is a big problem. For twenty percent of the population in L.A, life can be very hard. Many of them work in low-paid jobs in restaurants, hotels, hospitals, and stores. A lot of them live in unhealthy apartment buildings; others cannot find jobs. However, the city spends tens of millions of dollars to give people a place to live, and the number of homeless people has been going down since 2007.

Chicago

Chicago, Illinois, has a population of almost three million. The Windy City is on Lake Michigan, one of the five Great Lakes. When the Illinois and Michigan Canal[66] was built in 1848, it gave the area a water route from the Great Lakes to the Mississippi River. When trains began moving goods[67] across the country, Chicago became a very important center for all of the goods trains in the Midwest.

Today, Chicago is an important financial and banking center with many tall skyscrapers. It is also an important center for education. With eighty-eight libraries and more than thirty universities, it is home to some of the best research[68] centers in the country, including the University of Chicago, the University of Illinois at Chicago, and Northwestern University.

Chicago: Important Dates

1871	1885	1940s	1973	2008
Great Chicago Fire left 100,000 people homeless.	World's first skyscraper—Home Insurance Company—was built (55 meters tall).	Chicago's famous deep-dish pizza was created.	Sears Tower (now called the Willis Tower) tallest building in the USA was built (442 meters tall).	Barack Obama spoke to crowds in Grant Park after he was voted the 44th president of the USA.

Houston

Houston, Texas, is the fourth largest city in the USA. It receives over nine million visitors every year. There is a large student population, because the city has fourteen universities and colleges and one of the country's best research centers for medicine. Houston is famous around the world for its work in space exploration.

The Johnson Space Center, built in 1961, is the center of the country's space exploration program called NASA (National Aeronautics and Space Administration). The center had great success when the Apollo program sent the first man to the moon on July 20, 1969. The space center continued exploration with the Skylab, Apollo-Soyuz, and Shuttle programs.

Houston is very hot in summer, so the city has built eleven kilometers of tunnels under the city streets, where people can walk comfortably from stores to restaurants to businesses.

Washington, D.C.

The White House, home of the US president

The country's capital city, Washington, D.C., is named after the first US president, George Washington. It is on the Potomac River between Maryland and Virginia, and it is different from all other American cities because it is not in one of the fifty states. When Washington, Jefferson and other colonial leaders were deciding where to put the capital, they decided it could not be in one of the states, so they put it on land they called the

District of Columbia (D.C.). It is not one of the largest cities, but it is very important.

The White House on Pennsylvania Avenue is the home of the US president and his family, and Capitol Hill is the home of the US government.

The United States Capitol Building, home of the US government

The National Mall is the center of the capital city. It is a large open area with memorials[69] to some of the nation's famous presidents, and receives about twenty-four million visitors every year. The Martin Luther King, Jr. Memorial is one of the newest memorials, and the only one for a person who was not a president.

It was in Washington, D.C., at the Lincoln Memorial, that Dr. King gave his famous "I Have a Dream" speech in 1963. On the 4th of July, thousands of people watch the fireworks between the Washington Monument and the Lincoln Memorial.

Philadelphia

Another city that is very important in the country's history is Philadelphia, Pennsylvania. It is the fifth largest city in the USA, with a population of about one and a half million. It was the capital city during the American War of Independence, and the Declaration of Independence was signed there. Today it is a national center of law, with seven important law schools. The first hospital in the American colonies was built there by the British, and the city is still an important research center for medicine today. The name Philadelphia comes from Greek and it means "brotherly love."

Boston

Boston, Massachusetts, has a population of almost 618,000. Massachusetts is one of the six New England states in the northeast which were so important in the country's fight for independence. Boston is also one of the country's most important centers of education, with more than one hundred colleges and universities. Harvard University, one of the country's best universities, is just across the Charles River, in Cambridge, Massachusetts.

Irish immigrants settled in Boston in large numbers, and today make up 15.8 percent of the population.

Tourists enjoy visiting Boston's historical sights like Faneuil Hall, where the colonists met to plan the nation's fight for independence. The city is also home to some of the country's best sports teams, including the Boston Red Sox baseball team.

The USA is a large country, but most of the population lives on either the west coast or the east coast. The most populated state, California, has over thirty-seven million people. In the south, Texas is in close second place with over twenty-five million. On the east coast, New York State has over nineteen million people, and Florida has almost the same number. But some large states, like Colorado, New Mexico, and Montana, have just five million, two million, or fewer than one million people living in them. Large areas of the country are still open land with wild animals and beautiful nature, very much like they were thousands of years ago before the settlers arrived.

5 Nature and the Environment

Mount McKinley in Alaska is the highest point in North America.

The USA has five main geographical areas: the Northeast, the Southeast, Central, the Southwest, and the West. Together they make up the mainland, or continental, USA, with its forty-eight states. In 1959, Alaska and Hawaii joined the USA as its 49th and 50th states. These two states are not joined to the rest of the USA. Alaska, the largest state, is in the far northwest of North America, north of Canada. Hawaii is a group of volcanic[70] islands in the middle of the Pacific Ocean, west of California.

Climate

The climate on the mainland changes as you travel north to south and east to west. The Northeast has four very different seasons, with very cold, snowy winters and hot, humid[71] summers. In spring, the temperature begins to rise and the rainy season starts. In the fall, as the temperatures drop, the leaves on many trees change from green to bright red, orange, and yellow.

In the Southeast winters are mild[72] and short, while summers are long and hot. Oranges, lemons, and grapefruits grow in Florida's tropical[73] climate. The Central states are even colder and snowier in winter than the Northeast; they are hotter in summer and have heavy rainfall in spring. The Southwest is the hottest and driest area of the country with mild winters. Death Valley, in the Mohave Desert[74] in the states of California, Nevada, Utah, and Arizona, can get hotter than 49°C. In the far West, the wettest area of the country, thick forests grow in Washington state and Oregon.

Alaska's highest point is Mount McKinley, and its lowest is at sea level. In the north of Alaska, in the Arctic Circle, winters are very long and cold, so snow stays on the ground almost all year. The southeast of Alaska is the wettest area in the state, with milder temperatures.

The State of Hawaii has a tropical climate, and is made up of hundreds of islands in a chain, or line, that is over 2,400 kilometers long. The state has six main islands, and the island of Hawaii is the largest. Its tallest volcano, Mauna Kea, is 4,205 meters high.

Oceans and rivers

Ten thousand years ago, oceans and rivers brought the first Native Americans to the continent, followed much later by European explorers. From the Atlantic Ocean on the east coast to the Pacific Ocean on the west, to the Gulf of Mexico in the south, people used the rivers between these large oceans to travel, trade, and to have water to drink and fish to eat; these rivers are still important today.

Main Rivers	Length	From/To
Missouri River	4,023 kilometers	Rocky Mountains/Mississippi River
Mississippi River	3,765 kilometers	Allegheny Mountains/Rocky Mountains
Rio Grande	3,034 kilometers	Colorado/Gulf of Mexico
Colorado River	2,333 kilometers	Rocky Mountains/Gulf of California

5

Animals

Before Europeans settled in the USA, there were no urban areas. There were only forests, grasslands, mountains, deserts, and rivers, all full of wildlife. Native Americans killed animals for food and clothes, but they killed only the number of animals that they needed. As the population grew and people moved west, more and more animals were killed. The number of large bison, (also called buffalo) on the Great Plains in Central USA fell from millions to only a few hundred by the end of the 19th century. Today, scientists and environmentalists—people who want to help the environment—are worried about the future of many North American animals. These include animals like the bison, cougar, jaguar, prairie dog, caribou, and polar bear.

cougar

caribou

jaguar

prairie dog

bison

National parks

Many people today believe that wild animals belong in nature and, while the USA has less wild nature than it did, there are still many protected, open spaces. National parks have been created to take care of very large areas of wild land, and to protect the plants and animals living in them. Yellowstone National Park, in the states of Wyoming, Montana, and Idaho, became the country's first national park in 1872. It is home to many large, wild animals including grizzly bears, wolves, bison, moose, and elk. Yellowstone is famous for its large coyotes, which are a kind of wild dog.

5

The Grand Canyon in Arizona has been a national park since 1919. Over 1.5 thousand plant species are found there, as well as many diverse animal species, including 355 different kinds of bird and seventeen types of fish. Over thousands of years, the Colorado River has cut a canyon 1.6 kilometers deep, 446 kilometers long, and 29 kilometers wide. The Grand Canyon attracts about five million visitors every year. Visitors with strong legs can walk from the forests at the top to the desert basin near the bottom. Others can enjoy river trips on boats that go through the canyon. But most people drive to one or two areas at the top of the Grand Canyon and look out across one of the most beautiful places in the country.

Yosemite National Park, which is 320 kilometers from San Francisco in California, is visited by around 3.5 million visitors every year. It is home to a large number of plant and animal species. Within the park are many lakes, streams and waterfalls[75], as well as thousands of hot springs and natural geysers[76]; Yosemite Falls is North America's tallest waterfall at 739 meters. The park's famous sequoia trees can grow up to twenty meters tall.

The Grand Canyon in Arizona

The Everglades in Florida, a national park since 1947, is a large area of wetlands like a slow-moving sheet of water. When settlers moved to this area, they started changing the wet land to dry land so that they could grow food. This continued for many years and much of the natural environment was lost. But today, the national park service works to protect the many animals, including frogs, crocodiles, alligators, raccoons, opossums, foxes, and deer.

An alligator

Niagara Falls is a very popular place with tourists. It is the second largest waterfall in the world, between Canada and the USA in New York State. This is where the Niagara River sends water from Lake Erie to Lake Ontario, which it has been doing for about twelve thousand years. Niagara Falls is made up of three waterfalls—the American Falls and Bridal Falls on the US side are 56 and 55 meters tall, and together they are 326 meters

5

Niagara Falls

wide. On the Canadian side is Horseshoe Falls. Fifty to seventy-five percent of the water in the Niagara River changes direction away from the Falls to the hydroelectric power[77] stations that supply more than one quarter of the electricity used in New York State and Ontario, Canada. Over ten million visitors come to Niagara Falls State Park every year. They take photographs of the Falls, and have to shout in order to hear each other over the loud noise of the falling water!

Far away from the mainland, the state of Hawaii welcomes tourists with a *luau*, a traditional outdoor feast with dancers to entertain them. The Hawaiian Islands are famous for their beautiful beaches and wonderful water sports. Hawaii's Volcano National Park, a national park since 1916, has two of the world's most active volcanoes—Kilauea Volcano (1,277 meters tall) and Mauna Loa (4,169 meters). In the park, tourists can walk on volcanoes, in deserts, and in rainforests.

Environmental problems

Because the USA is so large, most people drive or fly to visit different areas of the country. Many Americans rarely use public transportation like buses and trains; one result of millions of people burning fuel[78] over the past fifty or sixty years is the serious problem of air pollution[79] and climate change. The Environmental Protection Agency, or EPA, is a government organization that works to protect the country's environment.

Many of America's lakes, rivers, and oceans have been seriously polluted by chemicals. The EPA is working to stop companies from polluting them and is trying to change people's habits in order to protect them.

The US Department of Homeland Security, a government organization that works to protect the country's people and environment, stops visitors from bringing fresh fruit, vegetables, plants, some animals, and other things into the country. This is because plants and animals from abroad can create big problems for native plant and animal species. If a visitor from abroad gets off the airplane with an apple from home, that person may have to pay as much as $300 for their mistake.

But there is nothing the government can do to stop nature from creating very big problems. Storms, earthquakes, hurricanes, heatwaves and many more natural disasters[80] make life difficult, and often kill many people and animals in the USA. The natural environment in the USA is beautiful and exciting, but it can also be dangerous.

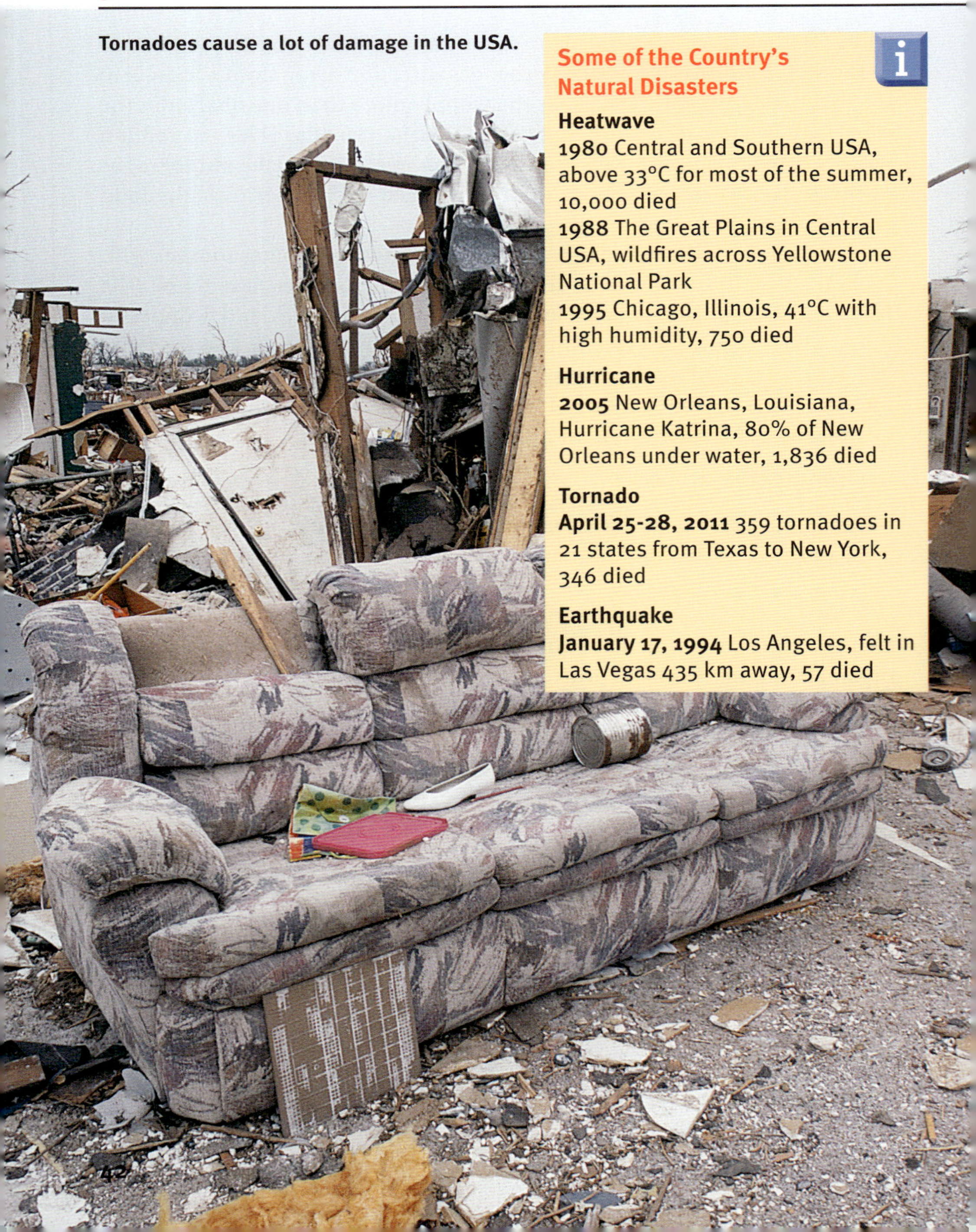

Tornadoes cause a lot of damage in the USA.

Some of the Country's Natural Disasters

Heatwave

1980 Central and Southern USA, above 33°C for most of the summer, 10,000 died

1988 The Great Plains in Central USA, wildfires across Yellowstone National Park

1995 Chicago, Illinois, 41°C with high humidity, 750 died

Hurricane

2005 New Orleans, Louisiana, Hurricane Katrina, 80% of New Orleans under water, 1,836 died

Tornado

April 25-28, 2011 359 tornadoes in 21 states from Texas to New York, 346 died

Earthquake

January 17, 1994 Los Angeles, felt in Las Vegas 435 km away, 57 died

6 Daily Life

The yellow school bus takes many students to school.

Many American school children and teenagers start the day by running out the door to get the school bus. Others walk to school, some drive themselves and their friends if they are old enough, and others are driven to school by their parents. Walking is better for the environment and for students' health, but it may not be possible, because some students have to travel long distances from home to school. In some rural areas of the USA students have to travel up to two hours to get to school. In towns and cities, the school bus meets students at a bus stop, but in rural areas, where houses can be far from each other, the school bus stops in front of each student's house. When a bright yellow school bus stops on a street or road, cars in both directions must stop until the students are safely on or off the bus and the doors are closed.

The school year usually starts after Labor Day in early September, and continues until the middle of June, so summer vacation is about ten weeks. Each school year has two semesters[81], with the first semester from September to December, and the second from January to June. The school day is Monday to Friday, usually from about 9 am to 3 pm. In most states,

American Schools

Age	Grade	School
5–10	K–5	Elementary
11–13	6–8	Middle (or Junior)
14–17	9–12	High

Note: grade K is Kindergarten for children at the age of 5

teenagers must stay in school until they are sixteen years old, when they can leave early, called "dropping out", to find a job. Students are usually around seventeen or eighteen when they finish high school.

There is no national curriculum in the USA. There can be differences not only between states, but also between towns in the same state. Public and private schools usually teach the same type of courses. Private schools, which are usually organized by churches, teach religion, but public schools do not. All schools teach courses like English, math, science, history, and geography.

At the start of the school day, middle and high school students go to their homeroom, the class where the teacher calls out each student's name. The school day always begins with students standing up, facing the American flag at the front of the classroom, putting their right hand over their hearts[82], and saying the Pledge of Allegiance, a promise to be a good citizen.

The hours in the school day are broken up into periods, usually forty-five or fifty minutes long. When the school day ends, many students stay after school to join extra-curricular activities, which are usually sports and clubs. Some popular extra-curricular sports include basketball, baseball, tennis, and volleyball. Students who do not want to do sports may join clubs, like French or Spanish club, math club, debating club, chess club, film club, theater, student government, school newspaper, choir, photography, or ski club. It is important for students to choose extra-curricular activities that they are interested in, and to put a lot of time and work into them. It is better to do only one or two well than to do a lot of them poorly. This is because colleges (the next stage of education after school) choose students not only for their grades, but also for their interests outside the classroom. The extra-curricular activities that a student chooses tell the colleges a lot more about that student.

Another extra-curricular activity is working on the yearbook, which is a book of photos of every student and teacher, school life, and sport events from that year. In high schools, it is often made by a group of students as an extra-curricular activity. Everyone can buy the yearbook at the end of the school year.

When students finish middle school and begin their high school education, they are called freshmen. In their second year, they are called sophomores, in the third year juniors, and in their fourth year they are seniors. For high school students who plan to go to college, there are special courses called Advance Placement. These courses let students see what college courses are like, and they can give them a good start to their college years.

Americans use the word "grade" not only for the year they are in at school, but also for the result they get for their school work and exams. When students get good grades, they pass; when they get bad grades, they fail.

Many schools use the letters A to F to give grades to students for their work and their exam results. In some schools, students need to get no less than 75 percent to pass. The students' grade point average (GPA) is the average of all the courses taken.

Grading

Grade	Percentage	Meaning	Grade Points
A	90–100%	Excellent	4.0 points
B	80–89%	Very Good	3.0 points
C	70–79%	Average	2.0 points
D	60–69%	Below Average	1.0 points
E/F	0–59%	Fail	0 points

When students fail a grade, like sixth grade, they do not continue their education with the rest of their class. They must repeat the whole year with the class who are a year younger. If a student fails two or three grades, they may not finish high school until they are nineteen or even twenty years old. These students sometimes decide to leave school, or drop out. There are over a million drop-outs each year in the USA. The number of teenagers who drop out of high school is greater in rural areas than in urban areas.

In the 1990s, a national organization called After-School All-Stars started after-school programs for middle and high school students living in poverty. Their goal is to keep children safe and to help them in school and in life. In 2002, the government passed a law called the No Child Left Behind Act. The goal is to make sure that every student finishes four years of high school with enough education to get a job and to have a successful life.

In American culture, most people see money as the route to[P] success, so it is no surprise that many American teenagers work after school, on the weekends, or both. Some teenagers work because their parents do not have enough money, but many teenagers work to buy things they want, like a cell phone or a new video game. Some teenagers want to save money so they can buy a car or go to college. Some children start earning money when they are eleven or twelve years old. Babysitting—taking care of babies and young children—is a good way for them to earn money. Cutting a neighbor's grass or washing cars are other ways they can earn money when they are too young to get a job. Each state has its own laws about when teenagers can start work. Without work experience, they can often get jobs in stores, hotels, and restaurants.

US Teen Facts

- 74% carry cell phones
- 42% can send text messages with their eyes closed
- The average teenager spends 31 hours each week on the internet

Many teenagers also work.

Some parents send their children to middle schools and high schools that have exchange programs, which means that they send their students to a school in another country for a semester or longer; students from the other country also come to the school in the USA. Exchange programs are an excellent way to practice a language, to meet new friends, and to learn about another culture. The student usually lives with a family that has a teenager the same age. Exchange programs usually offer scholarships to some students who cannot pay for the travel and living costs.

A very important and serious event in the school calendar is graduation. This is the ceremony at the end of the senior year, when seniors have passed all of their courses and exams, and have finished high school. June is the month for graduation ceremonies across the country. Boys and girls wear a long gown (a special type of coat worn for graduation ceremonies) and on their heads they wear a flat hat called a mortar board. Parents arrive at the ceremony to watch their son or daughter receive their high school diploma[83]. After the ceremony, parents may have a party with family and friends to celebrate. In the evening, the high school graduates usually have a big party, and they sign each other's yearbook next to their photo. They write things like, "You have been a wonderful friend and I will always remember you!"

Students at a high school graduation ceremony

Most high school students who plan to go away to college need to borrow money from a bank to pay for it. College is very expensive in the USA—students have to pay between $14,500 and $42,000 each year for four years. That does not include a room, food, books, and other expenses. But high school students with good grades, or extremely good athletes, may receive a scholarship—money given to them by an organization to pay for some or all of their college expenses. A sports scholarship has made a big difference to the lives of many young athletes by sending them to college where they can play their sport and study for free.

7 Sports

American football

> **"The Big Four"**
>
> NFL—National Football League (32 teams)
> NBA—National Basketball Association (30 teams: 1 in Canada; 29 in USA)
> NHL—National Hockey League (30 teams: 7 in Canada; 23 in USA)
> MLB—Major League Baseball (30 teams)

Team sports, like American football, basketball, baseball, and ice hockey, are very popular in the USA. American football is different from football played in other countries, which Americans call soccer. Hockey is mainly played in the northern states where winters are cold. High school coaches always look for really good players who may get a scholarship to a college or university. In the USA, a sports scholarship can be the start of a very successful career.

American football

The National Football League's seventeen-week season starts in early September. Half of the NFL's thirty-two teams are in the American Football

Conference (AFC) and half in the National Football Conference (NFC). Each team plays sixteen games, and, on average, over 67,000 fans go to football stadiums to watch each game. Each team wants to play on Super Bowl Sunday, but only the two best teams will play, and only one will win!

Many of the team names come from animals in the state, such as Indianapolis Colts (a young male horse), Miami Dolphins (a sea animal), Carolina Panthers (a large wild cat), and Arizona Cardinals (a type of bird). Other names come from an important industry, such as the Pittsburgh Steelers, where the steel-making industry was very important. The name San Francisco 49ers comes from the people who went to California in 1849 to find gold.

Famous AFC teams	
North	Cleveland Browns, Pittsburgh Steelers
South	Houston Texans, Indianapolis Colts
East	Miami Dolphins, New England Patriots
West	Kansas City Chiefs, San Diego Chargers

Famous NFC teams	
North	Chicago Bears, Detroit Lions
South	Atlanta Falcons, Carolina Panthers
East	Dallas Cowboys, New York Giants
West	Arizona Cardinals, San Francisco 49ers

Traditionally, American football has been a man's sport, but in the past few years, women have started their own football teams, such as New Hampshire Freedom, Philadelphia Firebirds, Houston Energy, and California Quake.

Football teams have a lot of players, but only eleven from each team play on the football field at one time. Making a touchdown by putting the ball past the other team's goal line is the way to score[84] points and win the game. Every player is important, but the quarterback—the player who throws the ball to his team—must be able to throw long and fast.

Football can be a dangerous game, and so the players wear helmets to protect their heads, and shoulder pads to protect their necks and shoulders. The number on each player's shirt represents his place on the team, like quarterback.

7

Basketball

While football players need to be big and strong, basketball players are usually thin and tall, and they have to be able to move very fast. Basketball is played in high schools and colleges across the country. The National Basketball Association (NBA)—the highest professional group—is internationally famous.

The Women's National Basketball Association (WNBA), which started in 1997, has twelve teams, including New York Liberty, Los Angeles Sparks, and Seattle Storm. Their slogan is "Expect Great." Women's basketball became an Olympic sport in 1976, and since then the US national team has won five gold medals[85].

LeBron James playing basketball for Miami Heat

Baseball

Baseball players are some of the most famous names in the USA. Babe Ruth, Joe DiMaggio, Willy Mayes, and Mickey Mantle are names known by every American from an early age. In 1927, Ruth, who played first for the Boston Red Sox team and later for the New York Yankees, could hit up to sixty home runs in one season. Sometimes a really good batter can hit the ball out of the ball park.

Two teams with nine players play on the playing field at one time. The pitcher throws the ball fast and the batter tries to hit it. When he does, he runs to first base, but if a player on the other team catches the ball and touches the base before the batter gets there, he is out. If the other team is still running for the ball, the batter runs to second base, and third base. When he gets back to home plate, he scores a point for his team. The team who scores the most points wins.

The World Series is the game played every year between the two best baseball teams in the country. Traditionally, the winning team visits the White House in Washington, D.C. and meets the president. The team gives the president a team T-shirt with his name on it.

Baseball words

base the three places the batter has to run to (first, second, and third base)

batter the player who hits the ball with the baseball bat

diamond the field on which the game is played

home plate the place where the batter stands

home run a point scored by the batter by running from home plate to first, second, and third bases and back to home plate without being stopped by the other team

out when the batter makes three strikes, he is "out" and another batter comes up to the home plate

pitcher the player who throws, or pitches, the ball to the batter

strike when the batter tries to hit the ball and misses

Ice hockey

A sport that is most popular in northern, colder areas of the country, like Rochester and Buffalo in New York State, is ice hockey, which Americans call hockey. In hockey there are two teams of six players on an ice rink for sixty minutes. Players use a hockey stick to push and hit the puck—a round, flat piece of rubber—across the ice. They score points by hitting the puck into the other team's net. It is a very fast game!

At the end of each season, which is from early October to the middle of May, the two best teams in the National Hockey League (NHL) compete for the Stanley Cup. The Montreal Canadiens, a Canadian team, have won the Cup more times than any other team, with twenty-four wins. The Detroit Red Wings have won it eleven times, which puts them in third place after another Canadian team, the Toronto Maple Leafs.

Canadian Wayne Gretzky is the greatest hockey player in NHL history.

Soccer

Another game that has excited people all around the world for a long time is football, which Americans call soccer. This sport is becoming more and more popular in the USA, and is now played professionally by men and women. In the 2010 World Cup, the US men's team won their game with Algeria 1-0. They tied with England 1-1 and with Slovenia 2-2. The USA won the 2012 FIFA Under-20 Women's World Cup in Tokyo, Japan. The best young players in the country are playing for clubs in the North American Soccer League and Major League Soccer.

8 Entertainment[86]

Above: Hollywood's famous hilltop sign   Top: Hollywood Boulevard

Hollywood in Los Angeles is the home of the American movie industry. It is world-famous, and Americans are very proud of it. Every year, millions of tourists visit the "Walk of Fame" on Hollywood Boulevard. This special sidewalk is covered in stars with the names of over 2,400 famous people, including actors, and people in television, radio, theater, and music. Marilyn Monroe, Marlon Brando, Matt Damon, Paul McCartney, and Elvis Presley are just some of the names there. Even Kermit the Frog has his own star.

Movies

At the end of the nineteenth century and into the early twentieth century, movies had no sound, and are known as silent movies. They were often comedies. The first movie with sound was *The Jazz Singer* in 1927. Silent movies became a thing of the past and "talkies"—movies with sound—became very popular. In the 1940s, Hollywood was making four hundred movies each year.

Every year, movie companies compete for the largest audiences[87], and every February, over thirty-seven million people watch the Academy Awards in Hollywood on TV. At this event, the movie industry celebrates the success of the past year. The winners receive a small gold statue called an Oscar from the Academy of Motion Picture Arts and Sciences.

Biggest money-making movies

Avatar (2009) $760,505,847
Titanic (1997) $600,779,824
The Dark Knight (2008) $533,316,061
Star Wars Episode IV: A New Hope (1977) $460,935,665
Shrek 2 (2004) $436,471,036

One movie star who is found on the Hollywood Walk of Fame is Meryl Streep. Many people say that she is one of the best actors of all time. She has been nominated by the Academy for an Oscar seventeen times. A nomination is when Academy members, who are other actors, say who they want to win. A number of names are nominated, and then the whole Academy decides who should get the Oscar. Streep has been nominated more times than any other actor in the history of the awards, and has won three Oscars. She won her first Oscar in 1979 for her part in *Kramer vs. Kramer* with Dustin Hoffman. She also won Oscars for *Sophie's Choice* (1982) and *The Iron Lady* (2011).

Steven Spielberg is one of the most successful directors[88] of all time. He has directed movies for more than forty years. He started in television in 1969. He made *Jaws* in 1975, which won three Oscars and made him a famous director. He has directed many famous movies, including *Schindler's List*, for which he won an Oscar for Best Director, *E.T.*, and *Saving Private Ryan*, for which he won another Oscar. Spielberg has won a great number of other awards for his directing, and his movies have made him a very rich man. But, more importantly, he is a much loved director all around the world.

Walt Disney and his wife with Mickey Mouse

Disney movies, including *Mary Poppins*, *Beauty and the Beast*, and *The Lion King*, are very popular with people of all ages. Walt Disney died in 1966, but people all around the world still know his name because of his famous cartoon[89] characters. When he was a young boy, he loved art, and he drew pictures of animals and nature. He enjoyed silent movies and entertaining his family and friends. At the age of twenty-one, he went to Hollywood and, in 1928, he created one of the world's best-known cartoon characters—Mickey Mouse. On November 18, 1928, the world's first cartoon with sound was seen at the Colony Theater in New York. Disney was the first to make cartoons in color and, in 1932, he won his first Oscar. Disney's first musical cartoon, *Snow White and the Seven Dwarfs*, was first seen in Los Angeles in 1937. After that, Disney made *Pinocchio*, *Fantasia*, *Dumbo*, and *Bambi*. By 1940, Disney had more than one thousand artists and story writers working for him, and his team had made more than one hundred movies.

Watching a movie in a movie theater is something people all over the world enjoy. But watching a movie at a drive-in theater is a very American experience. A drive-in theater is a large, open space where people can sit in their cars to watch a movie. The first drive-in theater opened in 1933. By the 1950s, there were more than four thousand drive-ins in the USA. Today, there are fewer than four hundred.

Theater

Many visitors to New York City enjoy going to a Broadway theater. Most people try to get tickets for musicals, such as *Chicago* or *Wicked*, which have a lot of wonderful songs and dancing. Entertainment with popular songs has brought large audiences to American theaters since the late 1800s, and audiences around the world love them, too.

The Antoinette Perry Award, also known as the Tony Award, is an award for Broadway theater actors, actresses, and directors. Since 1967, the ceremony has been in Radio City Music Hall in New York City every June. It is a great Broadway event with singing and dancing. Famous names from the movies, including Hugh Jackman, Whoopi Goldberg, and Daniel Radcliffe, have all entertained audiences on the night.

Popular Broadway Musicals

West Side Story (1957) Music by Leonard Bernstein, Lyrics by Stephen Sondheim
Chicago (1975) Music by John Kander, Lyrics by Fred Ebb
The Lion King (1997) Music by Elton John, Lyrics by Tim Rice
Wicked (2003) Music and lyrics by Stephen Holzman

Television

Most Americans own a TV and many people have more than one in their house. Americans like big TVs and a very large choice of TV programs. Three of the most popular TV studios are CBS, NBC, and ABC. Many people start their day with breakfast television, for example ABC's *Good Morning America*. Shows about family life became popular in the 1950s and continue to be very popular today. In the 1950s, these shows were about white, middle-class Americans. In the 2010s, TV shows such as *Modern Family* make clear the diversity in modern American families.

The biggest sports event on TV every year is the Super Bowl. Almost 80 million Americans watch the two best NFL football teams compete.

Most watched American TV programs of all time

1 *Seinfeld* (1989–1998) comedy
2 *I Love Lucy* (1951–1957) family comedy
3 *The Honeymooners* (1955–1956) family comedy
4 *All in the Family* (1971–1979) family comedy
5 *The Sopranos* (1999–2007) story (called drama) about the Mafia[90]

Music

American Idol is a very popular TV program where people who want to become famous singers compete. Carrie Underwood, one of the greatest female country singers today, became famous after being on the program. She has won many awards, including Entertainer of the Year. More country music is listened to than any other music in the USA, and its home is in Nashville, Tennessee.

America's many different ethnic groups have brought with them many different types of music. The African slaves brought their own music about life's problems and relationships, which was later called "the blues." Pop music, which is very popular today, came from the blues and from gospel music—religious music brought to America by the slaves. The famous American singer, Elvis Presley, listened to gospel music in church when he was a child in Memphis, Tennessee. He brought this to his rock and roll music, which greatly changed American music in the 1950s. He started his singing career in 1954, and by 1956, he was internationally famous. He won many music awards, and his music is still selling today long after his death in his home at Graceland in 1977. Another famous American musician is Eminem, whose rap and hip-hop music has made him one of the best-selling singers in the world.

There are a great number of famous American entertainers, but one name that everyone around the world knows is Michael Jackson. He was born in 1958 and died in 2009. Jackson started singing professionally at the age of five, along with four of his brothers, in a group called The Jackson Five. Songs like *ABC* and *I Want You Back* were number-one songs in the USA and elsewhere. In 1979, he left his brothers because he wanted to do things his own way. In 1982, his album[91] *Thriller* became the biggest-selling album of all time. His music videos of *Thriller*, *Billy Jean*, and *Beat It* changed the music video business completely. Jackson became extremely successful and young people everywhere tried copying his dance moves.

> The 1983 video for *Thriller* was fourteen minutes long and cost half a million dollars to make.

Another American singer known internationally is Madonna, who was born in 1958. She has had more videos played on MTV (Music TV) than any other singer. Her first album came out in 1983, and since then she

Michael Jackson

has sold more than 300 million albums worldwide. She was the best-selling female singer of the twentieth century. It is no surprise that she is in the "Rock and Roll Hall of Fame," a museum in Cleveland, Ohio, that celebrates the best rock and roll musicians. She won a Golden Globe Award for her part in the movie *Evita* in 1996, and was the director of the 2012 movie *W.E.*

Literature

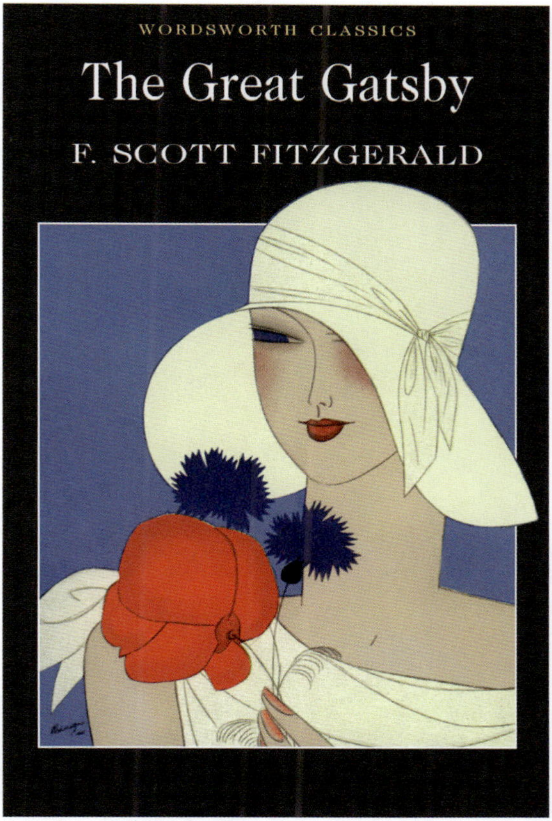

Many stories are about people living the American Dream.

American movies and theater plays have often been stories about people living the American Dream, and they have often been taken from novels by American writers. F. Scott Fitzgerald's novel *The Great Gatsby* (1925) is a good example of this. It is about an ordinary man looking for success by meeting the right people who can help him rise and get richer. John Steinbeck's *Of Mice and Men* (1937) is another novel of this type that was made into a Hollywood movie. And the American Dream is central to the play *Death of a Salesman* (1949) by Arthur Miller.

Every year, hundreds of literature awards are given to American writers. The American Academy of Arts and Letters gives seventeen awards every year. There are awards for literature by, or about, Americans of different ethnic backgrounds, such as the Arab–American Book Award, the Asian–American Literary Award, and the Hispanic Heritage Award for Literature. As in other countries, some of America's favorite writers have become national heroes.

9 American Heroes

Pochohontas in England, in 1616

A hero is a person who other people admire[92] because he or she is special or brave. People like George Washington, Benjamin Franklin, Sitting Bull, and Michael Jordan are American heroes. Heroes may be special people in history, entertainment, sport, or other areas.

Early heroes

One of America's earliest heroes is Pocahontas, a young Native American girl who lived in the early 1600s, and who helped the colonists in Jamestown, Virginia. She saved the life of an English soldier and colonist when her father, the tribe's leader, tried to kill him. The relationship between her tribe and the colonists got worse when the Native Americans carried away some of the colonists. The other colonists decided to take and keep Pocahontas. In the colony, Pocahontas became a Christian and, in 1614, she married a successful English tobacco planter, John Rolfe. The marriage helped to end the problems between her tribe and the colonists. In 1616, she was taken to London, England, where she met King James the First. She is remembered as a great friend to America's colonists in Virginia, and there are many books and movies about her life.

Johnny Appleseed was not the man's real name, but he was a real person. John Chapman was a successful apple grower in Ohio. He died in the 1840s, but stories about him grew into the legend of Johnny Appleseed. It is said that Johnny spent his life walking without shoes and in old clothes across the states of Ohio, Indiana, and Illinois planting apple trees. This kind and generous man loved everything in nature. He was loved by animals and admired by both settlers and Native Americans. In some places in Massachusetts, Ohio, Indiana, and Illinois today there are memorials to Johnny Appleseed. There are also celebrations for Johnny Appleseed Day, and even a Johnny Appleseed Museum.

Daniel Boone loved adventure and discovered new areas of land in Kentucky. He opened up new roads so that people could travel further west. He was the leader of a Kentucky settlement, and he also became an important leader in the state government. Many of the stories of his adventures include surviving long, cold winters, killing wild animals, and fighting Native Americans. In movies and TV programs about Daniel Boone, he is always seen wearing a raccoon fur hat, called a coonskin cap, which was worn by the Native Americans in Kentucky. These coonskin caps became a symbol of the great frontiersmen, and are still sold today to children who want to dress like American frontiersmen for Halloween.

Daniel Boone

Born: November 2, 1734
Died: September 26, 1820
Career: Explorer in the Appalachian Mountains in Virginia, Tennessee, and Kentucky; fur trader
Written about: 1826 James Fenimore Cooper wrote about Boone's experiences with Native Americans in *The Last of the Mohicans*

Davy Crockett lived from 1786 to 1836, and is known as the "King of the Wild Frontier." Crockett was a very good speaker and, in 1821, the people of Kentucky voted for him to represent them in the state government. In 1827, they voted for him again to represent Tennessee in the national government in Washington, D.C. Crockett was killed in Texas in a fight between the Mexicans and a small group of Texans at a place called The Alamo. The Texans were fighting for independence from Mexico, but they lost a battle[93] on March 6, 1836. The men who died there that day became symbols of America's fight for freedom, and Davy Crocket became an American hero.

Political heroes

Not all heroes from the nineteenth century are frontiersmen. Some heroes from that time are men and women who fought for the freedom of slaves; others fought for equal rights for women; others worked hard to start new organizations to help make people's lives better.

One of the many heroes from the nineteenth century was the sixteenth president of the United States, Abraham Lincoln. Lincoln was president from 1861 to 1865, the years of the Civil War.

Abraham Lincoln was born in Kentucky in 1809. His father was a farmer, and Lincoln spent his early life working on the farm. He was very interested in learning, but he went to school for only a few years. When he was twenty-one, his family moved to Illinois and he left home to get a job. He became interested in law, and taught himself by reading books. He was a successful lawyer in Springfield, Illinois, and then worked for the state government. In 1837, he spoke publicly against slavery. By 1850, slavery was against the law in the north, but not in the south. Lincoln became president in January 1861, and, when the southern states tried to leave the USA in April of that year, the war began. The southern states

19th Century Female Heroes

Elizabeth Cady Stanton (1815–1902) started her long fight for women's rights in Seneca Falls, New York in 1848. She worked to get women the right to vote.

Harriet Tubman (1820–1913) was an African–American who bravely helped slaves escape from the south to freedom in the north. It was very dangerous work, but she helped hundreds of people.

Susan B. Anthony (1820–1906) fought for voting rights for women and equal rights for all people.

Clara Barton (1821–1912) started the American Red Cross, an organization that helps people in dangerous areas.

Abraham Lincoln

wanted to keep slavery, even if it meant they had to make a different country of their own. Many people were killed in the long and terrible civil war, but in the end, the north won and slaves were free. At the end of the war, on the evening of April 14, 1865, Lincoln went to the theater. John Wilkes Booth, an actor who had wanted the south to win the war, went to the theater with a gun. There, Booth killed the president. Abraham Lincoln is remembered by many as one of America's greatest heroes of the nineteenth century.

Franklin D. Roosevelt, known as FDR, was the thirty-second president of the USA, from 1933 to 1945. When Americans voted for him in 1933, the country was going through the Great Depression, but he gave hope to the American people. After he became president, he created jobs and made new laws to change the way banks worked. His government made many more changes that made the USA a strong nation. He worked closely with the leaders Winston Churchill of the United Kingdom and Joseph Stalin of Russia in the Second World War. He worked very hard, and, by 1944, this handsome, tall man was very ill. The American people did not know that he was ill, and he won fifty-three percent of the vote in 1944. He died on April 12, 1945. He is the only American who was voted president three times. He is remembered as one of the best presidents that the country has ever had.

Civil rights leaders—men and women who fought for rights for African-Americans—are heroes whose names are well known and remembered.

Martin Luther King, Jr. is one of those famous leaders. But not all heroes have been leaders. There are sometimes ordinary people who do something very brave. One ordinary African–American hero is Rosa Parks, who was born in 1913 in Alabama.

The 1950s were a very bad time for African–American people in Alabama and other states of the southern USA. One of the laws in Montgomery, Alabama, stopped black people sitting in the front half of its city buses. Martin Luther King Jr. wanted to change this law. On December 1, 1955, Rosa Parks got on a Montgomery city bus to go home after work, and she sat down in the middle of the bus in a place for black people. When more white people got on the bus, there were not enough seats for whites, so the driver told Rosa to go to the back of the bus. When she refused, the driver called the police, who took her away to prison. One of the civil rights leaders paid for her to be freed later that evening. King now had an ordinary person to represent the fight against this law. Rosa was a good, honest woman and many people in the community liked her. For 381 days after that, almost all black people in Montgomery, and some white people, refused to ride the city buses. As a result of this, the bus company lost a lot of money. On November 3, 1956, the law changed, and Rosa Parks became a symbol of civil rights for African–Americans.

President John F. Kennedy

John F. Kennedy was a war hero who later became president of the USA. In 1943, in the Second World War, Kennedy was on a US boat when it was attacked. The boat went down. Kennedy swam through dangerous water and helped the other men to get to land. On January 21, 1961, 43-year-old Kennedy became the second youngest president of the USA (the first was Roosevelt at age 42). On that day "JFK" told Americans, "Ask not what your country can do for you—ask what you can do for your country." Kennedy wanted the USA to be a world leader in sending people into space, and for the USA to continue to progress. He met leaders of the civil rights groups, including Martin Luther King, Jr., and he wanted to change laws to make life better for African-Americans. But on November 22, 1963, he was shot and killed by a man with a gun in Dallas, Texas. America had lost a great hero and a president that had given the country great hope for the future.

Space heroes

Many people say that the USA is a country where anything can happen. And, when Alan Shepard became the first American to go into space in 1961, the impossible was beginning to seem possible. After Shepard, other Americans went into space, and, on July 21, 1969, Neil Armstrong became the first person to walk on the moon. In 1983, Sally Ride became the first American woman to go into space, and Guion Bluford was the first African-American. All of the men and women in the space program are American heroes.

Inventors

Throughout American history, there have been many great inventors—people who make something for the first time. Some inventors become national heroes because their inventions make extremely important changes to their country and also to the world. The names of some of these inventors are internationally famous.

1741	1852	1873	1879	1888	1891	1903
Franklin stove[94]	elevator	jeans	light bulb	Kodak camera	movie camera	airplane
Benjamin Franklin	*Elisha Graves Otis*	*Levi Strauss*	*Thomas Edison*	*George Eastman*	*Thomas Edison*	*Wilber and Orville Wright*

One internationally famous American is Henry Ford. In the early 1900s, cars were only for rich people. Henry Ford wanted to make cars quickly and cheaply, so that more people could buy one. He was the first person to use an assembly line—a way of making things with many workers doing only one job. Workers stay in one place and put one part on the car as it passes by them.

In 1973, the National Inventors Hall of Fame opened in Akron, Ohio, to honor[95] American invention and creativity. There are now more than 460 inventors in the Hall of Fame. Today it is in Alexandria, Virginia.

Henry Ford

Born July 30, 1863
Died April 7, 1947
Career engineer
Owned Ford Motor Company in 1903

Members of the National Inventors Hall of Fame

John Harvey Kellogg (1852–1943) breakfast cereal

Douglas Englebart (1925–) computer mouse

Ray Dolby (1933–) Dolby sound

Stephen Sasson (1950–) Digital camera

Stephen Wozniak (1950–) Personal computer

Heroes in medicine

In medicine, there have been a large number of discoveries that have changed people's lives. In 1955, Jonas Salk discovered a vaccine[96] against polio—an illness that killed many people and left many more people unable to walk.

In the early 1960s, John Enders and his team at Harvard University discovered a vaccine against the very dangerous childhood illness called measles. When one child got measles, it was quickly passed from that child to another. About three to four million Americans got the disease each year, and, of those who got it, four to five hundred died. After the use of Enders' vaccine, measles became a thing of the past. In 2009, only seventy-one people in the USA got it, but in some countries today, measles is still a big problem.

Superheroes

During the Second World War, Americans had another hero—Captain America. But this hero was the invention of Joe Simon and Jack Kirby for

Marvel Comics in 1941. Captain America quickly became the best-selling American comic book "superhero" during the Second World War, and today he is seen as a true American hero.

Americans first read about Superman in 1938, in DC comics. The stories were by writer Jerry Siegel and artist Joe Shuster. Superman is honest, and he fights crime and anyone who is dangerous. He believes in freedom and the American Dream. He is stronger than an ordinary man and he can fly through the air.

Technology heroes

In 1975, Bill Gates and Paul Allen started their internationally famous company, Microsoft. They wanted computers to be in every office and in every home. The Microsoft Company has been very successful, and now people all over the world use its computers. In 1995 and 1999, Gates wrote two books, which were very popular. He gave the money that he got from those books to organizations that help people to use technology in education. Gates has become a very rich man, and has about $61 billion, but he believes it is important for rich people to help others. In 2000, he and his wife started an organization called the Bill and Melinda Gates Foundation. This organization gives about $800 million every year to help people in poor countries to live healthier, better lives. The Gates family has also given a lot of money to libraries so they can buy computers, and they have given millions of dollars to schools and universities. In 2005, they gave $15 million to the Computer History Museum in Mountain View, California.

Bill Gates

9

The first computers were large and difficult to use, but by the middle of the 1970s, they were getting much smaller and much easier to use. In April 1976, Stephen Wozniak and Steve Jobs started a new company, Apple Computer. The two friends knew that their computers could be successful, and they were right. After Wozniak and Jobs created the Apple I and Apple II computers, they were millionaires. By the age of twenty-five, Jobs had over $200 million. In 1986, Jobs bought a small group of computer artists from Lucasfilm for $10 million, and called this group Pixar. Pixar and Disney worked together on the movie *Toy Story*, which was extremely successful, and Jobs became even richer, with over $1.5 billion. When Steve Jobs died in 2011, his fans around the world joined together in celebrating his life.

Steve Jobs (1955–2011)

Some inventions made by Jobs and his team of engineers:

1984	Macintosh computer
1998	iMac
2001	iPod
2006	iPod video
2007	iPhone
2010	iPad

Steve Jobs

10 Looking Forward

The Dragon Spacecraft owned by SpaceX

The US government spends a lot of money on new ideas in a country where anything can happen. Americans are successful in making enormous changes, not only for people in their country, but for people around the world.

In many American homes, there are very large TVs, dishwashers, and refrigerators. In the future, it is expected that refrigerators will tell people when food, such as milk, is no longer good. People will use their cell phones to find out what is in the refrigerator, so they will not have to be at home when they write their shopping list. Changes to how people live will not only be inside their homes—holiday plans may change a lot, too.

When the first man went to the moon in 1969, few people thought that one day they might go into space, too. But, in 2001, a Californian businessman was the first tourist to go into space. He took an eight-day trip to the International Space Station (ISS)—the world's first research center in space. More and more people are interested in becoming space tourists, and, from 2013, they can go with Virgin Galactic—if they have $200,000 to spend!

In 2012, the US government started using private space companies to take goods into space. They chose a private Californian company, called SpaceX, to send five hundred kilograms of food to the ISS. Elon Musk's company, SpaceX, was the first to make this important change in space travel. Musk's dream is to give almost anyone the possibility of traveling into space. In the same way that Henry Ford made cars cheaper so everyone could buy one, Musk wants to make space travel much less expensive. In the future, more tourists will pay private space companies for this amazing experience. But space travel can also be dangerous, and the US government is working with space companies to be sure it will be safe.

US Space Travel Accidents

Year	Spaceship
1967	Apollo 1 (3 people died)
1970	Apollo 13
1986	Space Shuttle Challenger (7 people died)
2003	Space Shuttle Columbia (7 people died)

The car is the most popular vehicle for people who prefer to stay on Earth. In the twentieth century, the car became very popular in the USA, when it gave people the freedom to travel more easily. But as the number of cars grew, the number of problems grew, too. Now, scientists and engineers are looking for ways to change cars so that there is less pollution, fewer car crashes, and fewer cars on the roads. Engineers are working on building cleaner electric cars using batteries[97]. Hybrids are cars which use both gasoline and a battery, and they have become very popular in the USA. The American company, General Motors, is the world's largest car maker, and it is making hybrid cars, trucks, and buses.

But the car of the future is expected to be the driverless, or self-driving, car. Engineers in the USA and other countries are working on a car that will drive itself. Toyota Prius has used Google's driverless technology to make one of the first driverless cars. In 2012, Nevada was the first state to pass a law on the use of them. Car makers hope to start selling many of

The Chevrolet Volt hybrid car

these driverless cars by 2025. People will choose where they want to go, and their car will take them there. People who cannot drive, such as children or people who cannot see or move well, will have much more freedom. Parents will not have to drive their children to school; the car will take them! Cars cannot read, so computer scientists in Texas are working on new ways for computers and cars to "talk" to each other. The computer will tell the car when to stop and when to turn right or left.

Computers and technology are responsible for changing many of the ways people live, from how we listen to music to how doctors save lives. Researchers at Massachusetts Institute of Technology have discovered a faster way to take clear three-dimensional[98], or 3D, pictures inside the body. With technology like this, doctors can see more clearly where and what the problem is. Doctors can now look at a 3D picture of a baby inside its mother. They can see if the baby has any problems before it is born. In the future, people may be able to use 3D technology to copy their medicine using their computers at home. They will not have to go to the drugstore to get it. Technology is really changing the way doctors work and, as a result, people are living longer.

All of this new technology means that the USA needs more workers who know how to use it. So it is important for young people to stay in school and to get a good education. Americans need more students to study science and technology. Some people in the government want students to stay in school longer. And they talk about giving American citizenship to students from other countries who study in the USA and become professional workers. Many Americans want to bring jobs back to the USA, too. In the past ten years or more, many American companies moved to other countries because it saved money. Now, the US government is offering to help companies that stay in the country.

Studying science

In looking forward to the future, Americans can expect many more changes to the way they live. The world can be sure that the USA will continue to spend money on education in the sciences and technology, in medicine, and environmental studies. Americans are extremely proud of their heroes, their inventors, and their children, who will become future heroes and inventors. These people often repeat President Kennedy's words, "Ask not what your country can do for you, but what you can do for your country." Many people from around the world choose to go to live in the USA, and many of them work hard to make it a better place. So, as we look forward to the future, the United States of America will continue to be a very exciting country.

Points For Understanding

1

1 Why did Christopher Columbus call the native people “Indians”?
2 Why did Europeans ship Africans to North and South America?
3 Who went to North America on *The Mayflower*? Why?
4 Why did New Amsterdam become New York?
5 What happened at the Boston Tea Party?
6 What was the Declaration of Independence and why was it important?

2

1 Which ethnic group is growing the fastest in the USA?
2 Who lives on reservations?
3 In 2009, what proportion of marriages was between people of different races?
4 Why is it difficult to control the number of guns in the USA?
5 In which states were the richest and poorest Americans living in 2010?
6 Why do people who live in suburbs have to have cars?

3

1 Why is America’s Independence Day celebrated on the 4th of July?
2 What do Americans eat on Thanksgiving Day?
3 How do Americans celebrate Christmas?
4 What do Americans do on Memorial Day?
5 What do American kids receive on Halloween?
6 How is Martin Luther King, Jr. Day different from other holidays?

4

1 How much has New York's population grown between 1771 and today?

2 What is one of the biggest problems in L.A. and what is being done to help?

3 When and why was the Illinois and Michigan canal built?

4 Where is the Johnson Space Center? What is it?

5 Where is Washington, D.C. and why is it an important city?

6 Which city is called "Bean Town" and where is it?

5

1 Which two states are not joined to the rest of the USA and how are their climates different?

2 What were the national parks set up to do?

3 Where is the Grand Canyon and how big is it?

4 Where is America's tallest waterfall?

5 Where is Volcano National Park and why do tourists go there?

6 What does the Environmental Protection Agency do?

6

1 When does the school year start and finish? How is it divided?

2 At what age do children go to Middle School?

3 Why is it important for students to do extra-curricular activities well?

4 What happens if a student fails a grade exam?

5 What is a drop-out? What areas of the country have the greatest number of drop-outs?

6 What happens at a graduation ceremony?

7

1 What is a sports scholarship and how does it help young people?

2 How many football players are on the field at one time and what does the quarterback do?

3 Why is Michael Jordan famous?

4 What sport do the New York Yankees play and who was one of their most famous players?

5 Where is hockey most popular and why?

6 What is the difference for Americans between soccer and football?

8

1 What do tourists find on the Hollywood "Walk of Fame," and where is it?

2 What is an "Oscar?"

3 For which movies did Meryl Streep win Oscars?

4 What happens at Radio City Music Hall in New York every June?

5 What did Walt Disney do for the American entertainment industry?

6 What music was brought to America by the African slaves?

9

1 How was Pocahontas's life different from the lives of other Native American girls?

2 What did the Native Americans wear that later became a symbol of the frontiersmen?

3 What did Harriet Tubman do?

4 Which president is remembered for freeing the slaves?

5 When did the first American woman go into space and what was her name?

6 How did Henry Ford's assembly line change the car industry?

10

1 What did SpaceX first do in 2012?

2 How will tourists be able to go into space from 2013?

3 What is a hybrid car?

4 How will driverless cars change the way people travel?

5 Why do more students need to study science and technology?

Glossary

1 ***population*** (page 6)
the number of people who live in a particular area

2 ***successful*** (page 6)
a successful person does well in their career. The fact of being successful in your career is called *success.*

3 ***immigrant*** (page 6)
someone who comes to live in a country from another country

4 ***proud*** (page 6)
feeling happy about your achievements, your possessions, or people who you are connected with

5 ***tradition*** (page 6)
a very old custom, belief, or story

6 ***celebrate*** – *to celebrate something* (page 6)
to do something enjoyable in order to show that an occasion or event is special

7 ***parade*** (page 6)
a public celebration in which a large group of people moves through an area, often with decorated vehicles and bands playing music

8 ***fireworks*** (page 6)
objects that make loud noises and colored lights in the sky when they explode

9 ***team*** (page 6)
a group of people who play a sport or game against another group

10 ***discovery*** (page 6)
the act of finding or learning about someone or something that was hidden or not known

11 ***represent*** – *to represent something* (page 6)
to be a sign or symbol of something

12 ***colony*** (page 6)
land that is controlled by another country. The people who live in a *colony* are called *colonists.*

13 ***freedom*** (page 8)
the right or opportunity to do what you want

14 ***native*** (page 8)
native plants, animals, or people that have always existed in a place

15 ***settle*** – *to settle somewhere* (page 9)
to go to live permanently in a particular place. People who *settle in a place* are called *settlers.*

16 ***tobacco*** (page 9)
a substance that people smoke in cigarettes or pipes

17 ***religious*** (page 9)
relating to religion – a belief in a god or in gods, or a particular system of beliefs in a god or in gods

18 ***symbol*** (page 9)
someone or something that represents a particular idea or quality

19 ***government*** (page 10)
the people who control a country or area and make decisions about its laws and taxes

20 ***tax*** (page 11)
an amount of money that you have to pay to the government. It is used for providing public services and for paying for government institutions.

21 ***event*** (page 11)
something that happens

22 ***against*** (page 11)
used for stating who or what you are trying to defeat in a game, race, or fight

23 ***declaration*** (page 11)
an important or official statement about something

24 ***independence*** (page 11)
freedom from control by another country or organization

25 ***signed*** – *to sign something* (page 11)
to write your name on something in order to show that you have written it, or that you agree with what is written on it

26 ***equal*** (page 11)
having or deserving the same rights, status, and opportunities as other people

27 ***right*** (page 11)
something that you are morally or legally allowed to do or have

28 ***education*** (page 12)
someone's experience of learning or being taught
29 ***leader*** (page 12)
someone who is in charge of a group, organization, or country
30 ***democracy*** (page 12)
a country that has *democracy* – a system of government in which people choose their political representatives in elections
31 ***vice-president*** (page 13)
a politician who is next in importance after the president
32 ***protect*** – *to protect someone or something* (page 14)
to keep someone or something safe
33 ***brave*** (page 14)
able to deal with danger, pain, or trouble without being frightened or worried
34 ***tribe*** (page 14)
a large group of related families who live in the same area and share a common language, religion, and customs
35 ***race*** (page 16)
a group of people who are similar because they have the same skin color or other physical features, or because they speak the same language or have the same history or customs
36 ***ethnic*** (page 16)
relating to a group of people who have the same culture and traditions
37 ***voted*** – *to vote for someone* (page 16)
to decide something, or to choose a representative or winner, by officially stating your choice, for example in an election
38 ***suburb*** (page 17)
an area or town near a large city but away from its center, where there are many houses
39 ***gasoline*** (page 18)
a liquid fuel made from oil that is used for producing power in the engines of cars
40 ***earn*** – *to earn* (page 19)
to receive money for work that you do
41 ***poverty*** (page 19)
a situation in which someone does not have enough money to pay for their basic needs

42 ***lead*** – *to lead to something* (page 19)
to begin a process that causes something to happen
43 ***violent*** (page 19)
using physical force to hurt people or damage property
44 ***recorded*** – *to record something* (page 19)
to make a record of something that has happened, usually by writing it down
45 ***mayor*** (page 19)
the most important elected official in a town or city
46 ***display*** (page 20)
a performance for people to look at
47 ***harvest*** (page 20)
the activity of collecting a crop, or the time when crops are collected
48 ***born*** – *to be born* (page 20)
if something such as a new organization or idea is *born*, it begins to exist
49 ***pumpkin*** (page 20)
a large, round vegetable with a thick, orange skin
50 ***decorated*** – *to decorate something* (page 21)
to make something more attractive by putting nice things on it or in it
51 ***competition*** (page 21)
an organized event in which people try to win prizes by being better than other people
52 ***flagpole*** (page 21)
a tall thin pole, used for hanging a flag on
53 ***candy*** (page 22)
a sweet food made of cooked sugar or chocolate but not containing flour, or a piece of this
54 ***community*** (page 24)
a group of people in a larger society who are the same in some way
55 ***inspiring*** (page 24)
making people feel positive feelings such as pride and enthusiasm
56 ***slogan*** (page 25)
a short phrase that is used for advertising something, or for supporting someone in politics
57 ***sights*** (page 26)
interesting places that people go to see

58 ***urban*** (page 27)
relating to towns and cities

59 ***climate*** (page 27)
the climate of a country or region is the type of weather it has

60 ***distance*** (page 27)
the amount of space between two people or things

61 ***24/7*** (page 27)
all the time

62 ***museum*** (page 27)
a building where valuable and important objects are kept for people to see and study

63 ***hectare*** (page 27)
a unit for measuring an area of land, equal to 10,000 square meters

64 ***diversity*** (page 29)
the fact that very different people or things exist within a group or place

65 ***industry*** (page 30)
all the businesses involved in producing a particular type of goods or services

66 ***canal*** (page 30)
a man-made river

67 ***goods*** (page 30)
objects that are produced for sale

68 ***research*** (page 30)
the detailed study of something in order to discover new facts

69 ***memorial*** (page 32)
a structure that is built to remind people of a famous person or event

70 ***volcanic*** (page 34)
formed by *volcanoes* – mountains that force hot gas, rocks, ash, and lava (= melted rock) into the air through a hole at the top

71 ***humid*** (page 35)
hot and wet in a way that makes you feel uncomfortable

72 ***mild*** (page 35)
mild weather is warm and pleasant

73 ***tropical*** (page 35)
used about weather that is very hot, especially when the air also feels slightly wet

74 ***desert*** (page 35)
a large area of land with few plants and dry weather

75 ***waterfall*** (page 38)
a place where water flows over the edge of a steep place onto another level below

76 ***geyser*** (page 38)
a place where hot water and steam move very quickly and suddenly up out of the earth

77 ***hydroelectric power*** (page 41)
electricity that is produced using the power of water

78 ***fuel*** (page 41)
gasoline or diesel used to power vehicles

79 ***pollution*** (page 41)
damage to air, water, or land caused by the harmful effect of chemicals (natural substances and new substances produced by combining or changing them through the science of chemistry)

80 ***disaster*** (page 41)
something very bad that happens and causes a lot of damage or kills a lot of people

81 ***semester*** (page 43)
one of the two periods of about 18 weeks that the school year is divided into in some countries

82 ***heart*** (page 44)
the organ in your chest that pumps blood around your body

83 ***diploma*** (page 47)
an official document that proves you have successfully finished all the work in a course of study

84 ***score*** – *to score* (page 49)
to get a point in a game or sport

85 ***medal*** (page 50)
a small flat piece of metal that you are given for winning a competition or for doing something that is very brave

86 ***entertainment*** (page 53)
performances that people enjoy

87 ***audience*** (page 54)
all the people who watch a particular movie, read a particular book, etc.

88 ***director*** (page 54)
someone whose job is to tell the actors and technical staff who are involved in a movie, play, or program what to do

89 ***cartoon*** (page 55)
a movie or TV show made by photographing a series of drawings so that things in them seem to move

90 ***the Mafia*** (page 56)
a secret criminal organization that is involved in illegal activities, especially in the USA and Italy

91 ***album*** (page 57)
a collection of music recordings which are provided together as one recording

92 ***admire*** – *to admire someone or something* (page 60)
to greatly respect and approve of someone or something

93 ***battle*** (page 62)
a fight between two armies in a war

94 ***stove*** (page 65)
a piece of equipment that provides heat for cooking and for heating a room

95 ***honor*** – *to honor someone or something* (page 66)
to show your respect or admiration for someone by giving them a prize or a title, or by praising them publicly

96 ***vaccine*** (page 66)
a substance that is put into your body in order to provide protection against a disease

97 ***battery*** (page 70)
an object that fits into something such as a radio, clock, or car and supplies it with electricity

98 ***three-dimensional*** (page 71)
not flat, but able to be measured in height, depth, and width

Useful Phrases

do what they were told*—to do what you are told* (page 9)
to do what a person, law, or rule says that you must do

were better off*—to be better off* (page 15)
someone who is better off is in a better situation, or has more money

on the go (page 17)
very busy or active

on average (page 19)
used for talking about what is usually true, although it may not be true in every situation

Trick or treat? (page 22)
used for asking for candy at Halloween. A *treat* is something special that you buy or make for yourself or for someone else. A *trick* is an unpleasant thing you do in order to harm, or pretend to harm, someone.

play a trick on them*—to play a trick on someone* (page 22)
to try to make someone believe something that is not true, either as a joke or as a serious attempt to harm them

the route to … (page 46)
used for talking about a way of doing or achieving something

Exercises

Welcome to the United States of America

Which of these things does *Welcome to the United States of America* talk about? Tick the boxes.

food ☐ accents ☐ size ☐ money ☐

nationalities ☐ history ☐ geography ☐ sport ☐

History

Choose the correct word to complete the sentences.

1 The king and queen of **Spain / Italy** sent Christopher Columbus to find a western route to Asia.

2 Christopher Columbus was born in **Spain / Italy**.

3 Columbus thought he was in **India / Florida**.

4 Africans were sold to American farmers and they worked for **no / little** money.

5 Some of the first English people arrived at ***The Mayflower* / Plymouth Rock**.

6 The Native Americans' positive feelings about the settlers **changed / did not change**.

7 **Henry Hudson / King Charles' brother** gave New York its name.

8 King George the Third wanted the colonists to pay tax to the British government for **tea / water**.

9 The words "All men are created equal" were written by **George Washington/ Thomas Jefferson**.

10 The US colonists had a war against **Britain / France**.

11 **Washington / Adams** was the first president of the USA.

12 Lots of people in the **north / south** became rich because of farming.

13 After the American Civil War, **African-Americans / Native Americans** were free.

14 Sitting Bull as killed by **US soldiers / US police**.

Traditions and Holidays

Match the sentence starts on the left with the correct endings on the right.

1	The Declaration of Independence was signed in	a	in Times Square.
2	Thanksgiving Day started in	b	1621.
3	On New Year's Eve, a ball is dropped	c	when winter will end.
4	Groundhog Day tells you	d	Labor Day.
5	On Memorial Day people remember	e	1886.
6	There is a holiday from work on	f	5th May.
7	Columbus Day began in	g	1776.
8	Everybody goes to work on	h	all the soldiers who have died.
9	Mexico's independence is celebrated on	i	Martin Luther King, Jr. Day.

Cities and Sights

Write the cities in the box next to the correct information below.

Boston (B) Chicago (C) Houston (H) Los Angeles (LA)
New York (NY) Philadelphia (P) Washington DC (DC)

1 about eight hundred languages NY
2 the Getty Museum ....
3 Universal Studios ....
4 space ....
5 the Windy City ....
6 excellent sports teams ....
7 the White House ....
8 the old capital ....
9 Martin Luther King, Jr. ....
10 Harvard University ....
11 melting pot ....
12 almost three million people ....
13 is not in one of the 50 states ....
14 walking underground ....
15 a law centre ....

Vocabulary: Nature and the environment

Replace the underlined words with the words from the box.

canal ~~climate~~ desert humid mild tropical volcanoes waterfall

1 The ~~weather~~ *climate* in the USA changes from north to south and east to west.

2 The Northeast is very hot with wet air in summer.

3 Niagara has a very famous place where water changes level.

4 Hawaii has many mountains that produce hot gas and melted rock.

5 The winters in the Southeast are not cold.

6 Florida has very hot weather.

7 In 1848, they built a river from the great Lakes to the Mississippi River.

8 Death Valley is in one of the hottest places in the area which has very dry weather.

Vocabulary: Anagrams

Write the letters in the correct order to make words from the book.

1	LAPOPUTION	*population*	the number of people who live in a specific area
2	ARMTIMING		a person who comes from another country to live
3	COINLOST		a person who lives in a place which is controlled by another country
4	AELDER		someone who organises a country or group
5	EBIRT		a group of families who live in the same area and have the same language and customs
6	LESTREST		people who go to live in a different place or country
7	MEAT		people who play sport together against another group
8	COINTUMMY		people who live together in the same area in a country
9	MONGERVENT		a group of people who rule a country
10	ANICEDUE		people who sit together to watch a film at the cinema or a play at the theatre
11	CRAE		a group of people with similar physical characteristics and history
12	CIDERORT		the person who tells actors what to do in a play or a film

Complete the sentences using some of the words from the table opposite.

1 A very famous film .... is Steven Spielberg, who has made many successful films.

2 Barack Obama was the first African–American .... of the USA.

3 The first British .... arrived in the USA in 1602.

4 There are nine players in a baseball ....

5 The Sioux are a Native American ....

6 Washington was the first president and formed the first democratic .... of the USA.

Vocabulary: Adjectives

Match the words on the left to the definitions on the right.

1	equal	a	using physical force to hurt people or things
2	religious	b	being happy with things you or other people do
3	violent	c	dirty air because of chemicals
4	brave	d	very hot, wet air
5	proud	e	to have the same advantages as other people
6	humid	f	not being frightened in dangerous situations
7	polluted	g	wanting to win or be better than other people
8	competitive	h	to believe in a god or gods

Word Focus

Write the nouns for these adjectives.

ADJECTIVE	NOUN
1 equal	*equality*
2 religious	
3 violent	
4 brave	
5 proud	
6 humid	
7 polluted	
8 competitive	

Now mark the stress on the nouns and adjectives with two or more syllables.

Useful Phrases

Match the sentence starts on the left with the correct endings on the right.

1 The African slaves did	a tricks on each other.
2 The route	b average 78.2 years.
3 On April Fool's Day people play	c the go.
4 In the USA people live on	d what they were told.
5 American people are always on	e or treat?".
6 At Halloween children say "Trick	f to success is hard work.

Grammar: Active and passive voice

Write the active sentences in the passive, and the passive sentences in the active.

1 America was named after Amerigo Vespucci.

They named America after Amerigo Vespucci.

2 They took away the land from the Native Americans.

....

3 Many animals were killed.

....

4 They pay people different wages in different states.

....

5 They take the children to school by bus.

....

6 Students are taught about American history.

....

7 They gave the Statue of Liberty to the USA in 1885.

....

8 Hawaii welcomes tourists with a *luau*.

....

9 Three hundred forty six people were killed in tornadoes in 2011.

....

Grammar: Correct the mistakes

Every sentence contains a mistake. Underline the mistake and write the correction.

1 People has big dreams—they want to live "the American Dream".

2 Millions of persons watch the 4th of July fireworks on TV.

3 Franklin D. Roosevelt is the only American who is being voted president three times.

4 Life for the Pilgrims has been very difficult.

5 Much Pilgrims died because of cold weather and wild animals.

6 Thomas Jefferson borned in 1743.

7 Cities growed quickly in the north because of trade.

8 At Thanksgiving, people eat things like potatoes and pumpkins pie.

9 Winters in Alaska are colder Hawaii.

10 JFK is the president what said, "Ask not what your country can do for you."

11 The Grand Canyon is being a national park since 1919.

12 People cannot takes food into the USA from abroad.

13 Some students can drives themselves to school.

14 The school year usually start in September.

15 Women in the USA have start their own football teams.

Making Questions

Write questions for the answers below using the question words given.

1 How many *states are there in the USA?*

There are fifty states in the USA.

2 How many ....?

More than 300 million people live in the USA.

3 When ....?

Washington was born in 1732.

4 How many ....?

Jefferson had about 200 slaves.

5 What ....?

Franklin was a writer.

6 When ....?

Lincoln became president in 1861.

7 How many ....?

There are seven Sioux tribes.

8 Are ....?

No. The laws are different in each state.

9 When ....?

The French gave the Statue of Liberty to the USA in 1885.

10 How long ....?

The Missouri River is 4,023 kilometers long.

11 Who ....?

Pocahontas helped the colonists in Jamestown.

12 What ....?

Rosa Parks refused to move her seat on a bus.

13 What ....?

Steve jobs started the Apple company.

Pronunciation: Vowel sounds

Write the words with the same underlined vowel sound in the correct column of the table.

brave candy colony ~~community~~ equal fuel freedom honor humid leader native parade pollution ~~population~~ ~~poverty~~ right ~~sign~~ ~~tax~~ ~~team~~ tobacco tribe tropical vaccine violent

/eɪ/	/i/	/aɪ/
population	*team*	*sign*
/u/	**/æ/**	**/ɒ/**
community	*tax*	*poverty*

Macmillan Education
4 Crinan Street, London N1 9XW
A division of Springer Nature Limited
Companies and representatives throughout the world

ISBN 978-1-3800-4175-3
ISBN 978-1-3800-4110-4 (with CD edition)

Written by Coleen Degnan-Veness with Chantal Veness

First published 2013
This edition published 2019

Designed by Carolyn Gibson
Cover photos courtesy of Digital Stock (r), PhotoDisc/Getty Images (tl), Getty/Taxi/Getty Images (bl).

The author and publishers would like to thank the following for permission to reproduce their photographic material: Alamy/G.de Heus p53(insert), Alamy/Horizon International Images Ltd p30, Alamy/D.Hurst p6, Alamy/Imagebroker p40, Alamy/NASA Archive p69, Alamy/PCN Photography p48, Alamy/M.Seroni p23, Alamy/Visions of America,LLC p47; Alamy Stock Photo/Pictorial Press Ltd p24 **Corbis** p63, Corbis/Bettman Archive p55, Corbis/Design Pics Inc p21, Corbis/Fancy p17, Corbis/J.Hicks p53, Corbis/Poodlesrock pp10, 11, Corbis/S.Pope/epa p42, Corbis/A.Schein Photography p17, Corbis/VEM/WestEnd61 p39(tr), Corbis/T.Wilcox p29; **Digital Stock** pp26(caribou), statue of Liberty repeated on each page; **Dorling Kindersley** pp4, 5; **Eyewire** pp26(cougar), 26(prairie dog), 27(bear); **Getty Images**/Bloomberg pp67, 68, Getty Images/Moment/Busà Photography title page and p26, Getty/Photolibrary p46, Getty/Roger Voillet p8; **Getty RF** p26(bison); **Getty images** p42, Getty Images/dra_schwartz p43, Getty Images/E+/andipantz pp12-13, Getty Images/fotog p20, Getty Images/WireImage/Steve Granitz p58 **Getty Images Sport** p52; **Hulton Archive** p14; **John Foxx Images** p26(jaguar); **Image Source** pp28, 72; **Photodisc** p27(moose), 27(elk), 27(wolf); **Photographers Choice** p32; **Rex Features** p16, Rex Features/Back Page Images p50; **Superstock**/Age Fotostock p71, Superstock/Alaska Stock p34, Superstock/T.Till pp38, 39; **Time & Life Pictures** p64; **Wordsworth Publishers** p59.

Printed and bound in by Bell and Bain Ltd, Glasgow

without CD edition
2023 2022 2021 2020 2019
10 9 8 7 6 5 4 3 2 1

with CD edition
2023 2022 2021 2020 2019
10 9 8 7 6 5 4 3 2 1